The Ultimate Real Estate Agent Book

Real Estate Top Producers Share Their Secrets to Achieving Massive Success

Orlando Montiel

The Ultimate Real Estate Agent Book

Printed by:
90-Minute Books
302 Martinique Drive
Winter Haven, FL 33884
www.90minutebooks.com

Published in the United States of America

160224-003

ISBN-13: 978-0692678572
ISBN-10: 0692678573

For more information on 90-Minute Books visit www.90minutebooks.com or
call (863) 318-0464

Here's What's Inside...

Introduction

Success in real estate is very elusive. As agents, we start our businesses looking for money and flexible hours to do what we want to do, but all too often those dreams are dashed to pieces by the crushing realities and difficulties of being real estate professionals. There simply isn't enough time in the day to do everything we want to get done, and there doesn't seem to be enough resources to make it happen. Often, we find ourselves working late nights and during the weekends with very little money to show for it.

Financial hardship, irregular income, and mental and emotional fatigue are too common in this industry. The business of real estate can be very, very hard if we are not fully prepared to embrace the demands of such a rewarding yet competitive profession. The good news is that there is hope. You can conquer the chaos, you can have the business you always wanted, and you can have a great life. Many have done it, and there is no reason why you shouldn't be able to.

Over the past 15 years, I've personally coached and interviewed thousands of agents, and 30 of the top agents in the country including #4 and #7 according to Forbes and the Wall Street Journal and I discovered that they all do different things in different ways, but they all do the major things the same way.

What they don't do?

They don't do Cold Calls

They don't call expired listings

They don't work with For Sale By Owners

They don't just send postcards

What they do is 100X more powerful than ANY of those things. And even now, hardly anybody understands the strategy.

The following pages are filled with exciting stories and ideas from successful brokers and agents who are going to share with us what works and what it takes to build a successful real estate practice in today's crowded real estate industry. Our purpose at The Montiel Organization is to help real estate agents succeed by following a three-step process. First, increase profitability. Second, put in place systems to automate the business. Third, scale the practice to make more money and have more free time. These three steps are the reason our company exists.

Having worked with thousands of agents, we've seen consistent patterns among those agents that are successful and those that are not. In this book I have interviewed 12 of the most successful real estate agents and brokers in North America. They are in the top 1% of their peers in the nation, and they have consistently grown their revenues, profits, and positive reputations based on their uniquely valuable problem-solving throughout the marketplace. They increasingly transform the structures, relationships, and systems within their businesses. The insights they have all generously shared with me during our interviews for the Miami Real Estate Show are invaluable.

Enjoy the book!

I hope this book inspires you to take charge of your real estate career and encourages you to learn and implement the systems, strategies, and best practices that the most successful agents in North America use to grow their businesses. You can see the full video interviews at www.MontielOrganization.com/interview

To Your Success!

Orlando Montiel

Interview #1: Alicia Cervera Sr. and Alicia Cervera Lamadrid

Four decades ago, Alicia Cervera Sr. was crowned the Queen of Brickell, and today, with over $12 billion in sales, she has earned her title as the Grand Dame of real estate.

Cervera Lamadrid joined her mother's firm in the early 1980s, and by 1992, she was the youngest founding member of the Master Broker's Forum, where she currently serves as Honorary Chair. Most recently, she was recognized by the Greater Miami Chamber of Commerce as "2011 Condo Broker of the Year" and by the Miami Herald as "2011 Miami Power Broker".

The Alicias' record is impressive: over 45 years selling south Florida real estate and more than 100 exclusive projects sold, including over 45,000 condominiums.

Orlando: I want to get started with Alicia Sr. When did you come to Miami?

Alicia Sr.: In 1961, I arrived with my Cuban husband, who fled Cuba through the Mexican Embassy. We first went to Mexico, and then we moved to Miami.

Orlando: Alicia, what's your background?

Alicia: I was born in Cuba. Actually, my sister and I arrived in Miami just a few months before my parents. I had the privilege of growing up in three cultures because both of my parents are very strong individuals. My dad is Cuban, my mother is Peruvian, and, of course, I grew up in Miami in the United States.

Orlando: Alicia, when did you come into the industry?

Alicia: I came into the industry when I started chasing Mom as she was pacing lots. I was running behind her, and she was saying, "One, two..." to measure the distance. I was probably under three, four, five years old then.

Orlando: So you have real estate in your blood?

Alicia: It's all about real estate, but I got my license when I was 21. I was at the University of Miami, studying psychology, and my dad sat me down and said, "It's really nice that you're in school, and it's so important that you get your degree in psychology, but I don't want you to starve to death. You need to get a real estate license."

My dad doesn't have a lot of rules, but the rules he has have been clear, and I learned many years ago not to fight with him. So I got my real estate license mostly to get him off my back.

I was in the PhD program for Clinical Psych at the University of Miami, so I would work for Mom in the summers, part-time.

This is a beautiful business. It's a business with tremendous opportunities, and I've been lucky to grow up in a city that grew up with me. Ultimately, we folded into the business, and here I am.

Orlando: How many generations are working in the company now?

Alicia Sr.: Three generations.

Orlando: What lessons have you learned from the 1990s, then the 2000s, and during the current cycle?

Alicia: I think we learned different lessons at different times. In 2007 or 2008, I remember Mom looking at me and saying, "If the banks don't fail us, we'll be fine."

We were plodding along, and I was getting ready to close about 350 units in a building called 50 Biscayne. I had 50 closings scheduled in the morning when all of a sudden, the FDIC pulled all of the loans with Freddie Mac and Fannie Mae. They were all cancelled.

I remember sitting there and saying to myself, "I guess the banks just failed us." It was clear that it was the beginning of the debacle. I remember talking to the bankers and saying, "You have to come up with something. You have to show that you believe in the product, and you have to transform your construction land into the end users' money."

At that point, they told me that I was out of my mind. Ultimately, however, a year or a year-and-a-half later, that's exactly what they did. They stepped up and started giving loans to those buyers. That's when the closing started to happen.

Orlando: What did you learn from that experience that makes you a better businessperson today?

Alicia Sr.: I think it's very important to remain calm because when you are calm, you pass that spirit to your buyers.

Orlando: Exactly. What about you, Alicia?

Alicia: I learned to show up. For me, it's important to show up every day, and remember that each person is an individual with a particular unit in mind that was the world to them.

When you're representing thousands of units, which we were, it's easy to put everybody together and just throw the same formula at everybody. I learned that as important as it was to come up with options and potential solutions, it was just as important to listen to each person's story. Oftentimes, it was very painful because the stories were very similar, even though they came from different voices. Many people were very angry, other people were desperate, and we had to deal with this outpouring of human emotion that was very tough.

I definitely learned that you need to show up, you need to listen, and, as Mom said, "Stay very calm, and focus on the fact that they are human beings on the other side; they're not just numbers and contracts."

Orlando: What about a success story, one of the many you've had?

Cervera is a name associated with real estate in Miami. You help developed the city into what it is today. When you arrived in Miami, the zoning at that time was different, right? There was, I think, one building in the Brickell area.

Alicia Sr.: The laws would not permit high-rises in Brickell back in the 60s, so when the new law was passed, I thought it was a great opportunity. I talked to many developers, but I decided to write a letter to Harry Helmsley from New York, the most powerful man in real estate at the time. He was the owner of the Empire State Building, the Park Lane Hotel, etc. He was a billionaire when there were no billionaires.

I explained to him who I was, that I had lived in South America, and that it was worth looking at Miami. To my surprise, two or three days later my partner said that Mr. Harry Helmsley was on the line. I thought that my partner was playing a prank on me. I went to the phone, and the very professional voice of a secretary told me, "Mrs. Cervera, can you wait for Mr. Harry Helmsley, please?"

Everything started there. I had a meeting with him, and he hired me. The wife, who was already a powerful woman, took me aside and said, "You are going to have a great job." It was my first success because I got to work with the most important man in real estate.

Orlando: Many people in real estate are afraid to ask or are intimidated by a very powerful businessperson, when sometimes just asking is what gets the job done.

What did you learn from him?

Alicia Sr.: One day we had a problem where the city wouldn't give us a permit on a building. I called Harry, quite upset about it, and he said, "This is a little battle. We are going to win the war, so don't worry."

He was my great mentor.

Orlando: Did you learn any other lessons from Mr. Harry Helmsley?

Alicia Sr.: I learned to be very calm about business.

Alicia: Well, as a manager. It was quite an offer you got but I got some very good choices. We picked five people. We started the new company, and it was a tremendous run because obviously we did some amazing things with Jorge, and we sold thousands of apartments and made billions of dollars. It was a great journey, through which Related became what it is today. We sold, as I said, so much inventory, and for me it was an opportunity to grow astronomically because Mom was very busy running Cervera Real Estate and selling thousands of apartments with Veronica. I was running this other company. I had never wanted a company pretty much on my own because I certainly have Mom; they are backing me up and supporting me. Mom had her own company that she was running, and Jorge was a little busy running Related.

Orlando: What about you, Alicia?

Alicia: I learned that I was running this marketing organization, and it was huge lesson in so many ways.

Orlando: You said a keyword that struck me: marketing organization.

Alicia: Yes. As we all know, you can't sell anything that you don't market first. This is a sales and marketing organization. You have to identify what the product is and then communicate that.

Orlando: I completely agree with you. I say to the agents that we coach and train that we're not in the business of real estate; we're in the business of marketing, and real estate is the vehicle. We need to learn to become very good marketers.

Alicia: Without a doubt.

Orlando: What did you learn from working with the biggest developer in Miami, Jorge Perez?

Alicia: I learned not to be afraid and that with every challenge came an opportunity. There are never opportunities without challenges.

I learned by working with my mom that nothing is worth wrinkles. I would complain about something, and she would often tell me, "Nothing is worth wrinkles. If you can't do it with a smile, and if you're going to lose your feminine side and happiness, stop doing it." It was a great lesson.

With success, as I said, comes a lot of challenges. What we do is a hard job, and the more successful you are, the more challenging it becomes because with every opportunity comes challenges.

Orlando: You have more than 300 agents in your company, and you have worked with so many in the past. What characteristics make a great agent?

Alicia: I think that it's a combination of discipline and entrepreneurship.

Alicia Sr.: We have both the same answer.

Alicia: People are attracted to real estate oftentimes because of the freedom that it will lead to. Freedom is a wonderful thing, but only if you don't abuse it. In this business you have to show up every day. One of the challenges, especially at the beginning, is that people think that if they don't have any work to do, any appointments, or any showing, they don't have to go to work.

I always tell the agents when they are starting, "If you think you're going to make more money sitting at home than being in the office, go get another job because that's just not going to happen." If you're in the office, at least there is the possibility of an opportunity, so, at minimum, do that.

Then the entrepreneurship kicks in, and if you are being creative, you can't be afraid of trying anything. Do the things that seem obvious, but also do the things that don't seem obvious.

My mom told me when I got into this business, "If you want to be successful, you have to be the first one in and the last one out." I added to that with my daughter: "If it's not illegal or immoral, do it."

Orlando: Is there a daily practice that makes both of you very successful?

Alicia: It's going to be repetitive, but I show up every day. I am here even when I am not here.

In the old days, my practice was to finish every day; anything that's on my to-do list was finished. These days, you never finish because your emails come at one in the morning, two in the morning, three in the morning. You never finish, so I had to learn to not finish. It's a journey.

One of the difficult things that I had to do in order to grow personally in my business was to stop doing things that I liked doing because it wasn't the best use of my time. I had to give up a lot of things that I really enjoyed in order to take my business to the next level. What you do is going to change. At some point, you need to put the immediate and the urgent aside to deal with the important stuff.

You have to ignore the phone and that day-to-day business in order to sit back and put together a strategic plan that will really help you move forward.

I remember a story about Bill Gates as a child. He would sit in his attic for hours. His mother said that she would go nuts because he was sitting in the attic with the lights off. One day she finally couldn't take it anymore, so she went up there and said, "What are you doing?"

He said, "I am thinking, Mom. Don't you ever think?"

At that point, I was in a transition in my career, and I decided that I was going to take half an hour a day and just think. It's very difficult to turn off all the noise and just think, but that year I made more money than I ever had up until that point in my career.

Orlando: That's something we say to the agents that we coach: Every single day, first thing in the morning, plan your business; do it for just 15 minutes. It doesn't have to be more. If you do it every single day, you will have a very clear mind about where you want to go.

What about you, Alicia?

Alicia Sr.: Every night I write down four or five of the most important things the company needs. The next day, my assistant COO, who started with me as an assistant, calls me at 8:30, and I review those things with her.

Orlando: Every morning at 8:30 she reviews whatever you wrote the night before? What a great habit.

Alicia Sr.: If I don't do it, I can't sit well because those things are going to be jumping in my head. Once I put them on paper, then they stop jumping in my head.

Orlando: If you could give a piece of advice to a new agent, what would it be?

Alicia Sr.: To concentrate on an area that they like, to position themselves in a territory. Every time one of my agents follows that advice, they come to me at the end of the year and say, "Thank you for the advice."

Orlando: Alicia, I can't agree more. That's our first step in coaching: Position yourself in terms of the area where you are going to work. Position is extremely important.

What about you, Alicia?

Alicia: Once you do that, find the leader in that market, and go work for them for free. I say "for free" because it doesn't matter what you get paid or don't get paid.

I firmly believe that you get what you give. If you make yourself available to that person, you will end up getting much more than you give, so find a mentor.

Orlando: Find a mentor. It's much easier to ask, "Who?" than to ask yourself, "How."

Alicia: Yes, if you are with the right "who," you will find out the "how." I often say that if you can ask the right question, you'll always come up with the answer. It's harder to ask the right questions, and that's why mentoring works so well.

I also tell new agents and old agents to remember that part of something is so much better than all of nothing. I think, oftentimes in business, people get stuck with not wanting to share. It's an enormous mistake.

Orlando: What advice would you give to top producers?

Alicia: Mom talked about thinking outside of the box, and I think that's critical. No one does that better than Mom, but it's not only about thinking outside of the box; it's about getting outside of your comfort zone.

Whenever you are comfortable doing what you're doing, that's a huge red flag that you need to be doing more. As soon as you get comfortable, figure out how you can make yourself uncomfortable because that's where you grow up. Oftentimes, that means believing in yourself. You have to know that you can afford an assistant, marketing budget a vacation, or that you should try a different model.

Also, don't ever assume that what you're doing now that has created your success is going to create your success in the next season, in the next cycle, or in the next year. You have to be reinventing yourself and constantly looking for your business opportunities. When you are in this cycle, think about what's coming next and how you are going to be successful in that time.

Orlando: I can't thank you enough for this opportunity to interview both of you at the same time.

Alicia: Thank you for your interest and the opportunity.

Interview #2: Anthony Askowitz

RE/MAX Advanced Realty broker-owner and top producer, Anthony Askowitz.

Anthony was the number-one broker in 2008 and 2011 for the state of Florida for RE/MAX North America. He is the owner of the number-two office in terms of production for the state of Florida in RE/MAX North America. Anthony has gone from 100 transactions per year to 170 transactions per year, and he is a member of the master broker forum.

Orlando: Welcome, Anthony! How long have you been in the business, what is your background, and why real estate?

Anthony: I got my real estate license in 1989. I was 22 years old, had just graduated from college, and really had nothing else to do.

I applied for my substitute teacher's license, but the real estate exam happened first. I interviewed six different real estate companies, chose one, got great training, and the rest is history. I have been with RE/MAX for 25 years.

Orlando: You have won many awards, among them, Number One Broker in Florida for RE/MAX in terms of volume, Number Two Office in Florida for RE/MAX in terms of production, Number Six Producer in Florida with over $60 million in sales.

You also belong to the RE/MAX Diamond club, which means that you make more than $1 million in commission per year. That's very, very impressive.

How did you get to this point? Did you have a mentor when you got started in the business?

Anthony: I'm a firm believer in coaching. My first coach came in 2002. I had hit a plateau, albeit a pretty good plateau. I couldn't get over selling 100 homes in 1 year.

Ultimately, I sought out a coach, I engaged with him, and I was able to go from 100 transactions to 170 transactions.

Even to this day, I have always had a coach, going on 38 years. The bottom line is, with coaching, I get better. There is always something that you can tweak, and it's always made a huge difference in my business and my life.

With my coach in 2002, my business increased by 70%. I went from 100 transactions to 170 transactions. You learn to work smarter!

Orlando: What are the key lessons you learned from that experience of going from 100 to 170 transactions in 1 year?

Anthony: I was able to stop working with buyers and let my team members to take over those slots. My coach showed me that you work with an average buyer for 32 hours and with sellers for about 8.

Orlando: We need to learn how to delegate.

Anthony: It is delegation. It's also about living one's life. If I didn't have a team, I couldn't go away and feel comfortable about going away. I want to go away; that's part of living one's life, and that's one of my goals for everyone out there in real estate. You should be able to leave.

Orlando: When we were talking off-camera, you were telling me about the importance of farming. Can you elaborate on that?

Anthony: Generally, people think of a farm as a geographic area. Actually, farming is so much greater than that. Farming is a geographic area, farming is one sphere, and farming is working with foreclosures. Farming is any way you can get business, whether it's with doctors or lawyers. Farming is so many different things. You want to have streams of income. As a top producer, I have different streams of business. If one is not working as well, it's okay because I have other streams that will continue to do well! I do geographic farming.

I say to my agents, "Concentrate; focus on your sphere of influence. What is the average time someone sells their house?"

They say, "Five, seven years."

I say, "What if it's 10 years? If you know 100 people, that's 10 listings a year, 10 sales." That is almost one sale per month.

Orlando: How do you target your sphere of influence?

Anthony: Facebook is an easy way. It's free. Email is free, and the phone is amazing and also free. You have to touch your sphere in different ways.

You spend $20. You have to invest in your business.

Orlando: What tips can you give to an agent about making a solid, successful presentation?

Anthony: They have to be prepared. There is no excuse, in my opinion, not to be ready. Being prepared is part of being in business. You can't be a fake agent; you need to be prepared.

Orlando: How do you prepare yourself?

Anthony: I do it in different ways. First of all, I have my listing package ready to go. I can pull it off the shelf, and I am ready to go at a moment's notice. For example, there is not a day that you will ever catch me wearing jeans because I never know when business is going to call, and I have to be ready.

Also, it does not matter what has happened to me that day. When I walk into the door, the seller does not care what happened to me during my day. It's all about them. I need to be ready and focus.

As far as statistics and numbers, I don't use much when I'm going on a listing presentation. I give them what has sold, and I show them what's actively for sale and what's pending. It's a short and fast presentation; the shorter and the faster is better for the client and my business.

I'm the broker of RE/MAX Advanced Realty, and I have 150 amazing associates and two offices.

Orlando: As the owner/broker of RE/MAX Advanced Realty, you manage over 150 agents. What are the common problems that agents face today?

Anthony: Fear. They are afraid to make a phone call. Fear is an incredible motivator. The fear of not to being able to eat is a great motivator. There's also the fear of being successful. I think once they let go of the fear, they can be much more successful.

Orlando: We say in coaching that fear is your friend. It is an indicator, sometimes, of the things you should not do, but, more often, it's an indicator of the things you should do.

We explain to the agents in our coaching program that they are not selling real estate; they are selling confidence. Anybody can show a property, and every agent has access to the same inventory. The number-one reason a client goes with an agent is TRUST.

Anthony: People often think that time is equal to money, but time is not equal to money. You can't get your time back, and that is so important to recognize. When you go on that listing presentation, you have to hit a home run. Once you get up to bat, you have to be successful, or you lose your time, and you're not making any money.

Orlando: Is there any particular failure of yours that stands out, and what did you learn from it?

Anthony: I have plenty of failures. I think anyone who says they don't is a liar.

Orlando: Or they are not successful.

Anthony: One of my biggest errors was that I kept team members on the team for way too long because I thought that I could change them. I learned that over time, you hire better. If you get someone for $10 an hour, which is not me, you get a person, but getting a person doesn't mean getting a good person. Sometimes paying a little bit more makes a huge difference. I caused a lot of damage to my business and my own psyche before I learned this key point.

I thought I could change people, but that's not possible. You can't change someone. Surround yourself with incredible people. That's what has allowed me to grow to where I am today.

Orlando: What did you learn from your success stories?

Anthony: My first success goes back to before 2002, when I hired my first assistant. The first thing that elevated my business was hiring someone to organize me. She put things in place for me. I understand that I need A and B to make money.

It's the same in my house. I don't clean my pool, and I don't cut my grass. I have kids, and I would rather spend time with them doing other things.

Orlando: You have three businesses, 150 agents, you're a top producer, and you have a family business. What method do you use to relieve stress?

Anthony: I play tennis three to four times a week. I work out every once in a while, but I also live my life. I won't say, "God forbid I drop dead today, I didn't live my life." I love to travel. I go away every single month, even if it's just for the weekend, and I will continue to do so. Everyone has to find what makes him or her happy, but tennis is very important for me.

Orlando: If you could give one piece of advice to a new agent, what would it be?

Anthony: Set up systems in your business. Put everything in place, and get it done now. You will reap the benefits tomorrow. If you plant the seeds today, in six months to one year, you will see the benefits of what you did today. Don't take shortcuts. Do it, and you will be much more successful down the road.

Interview #3: Craig S. Studnicky and Philip J. Spiegelman

Craig Studnicky and Philip Spiegelman are the founders of International Sales Group (ISG) and the makers of the *Miami Report*, a MUST-read publication for every real estate agent and potential buyer.

Since founding ISG, Spiegelman and Studnicky have been responsible for more than $8 billion in sales and for leading developers including Jorge Perez (Related Group), Kevin Maloney (Property Markets Group [PMG]), and Donald Trump, among others.

ISG currently represents the following projects on an exclusive basis:

Muse, Echo Brickell, Downtown Doral, Echo Aventura, W Fort-Lauderdale, Sage Beach, The Crimson, Mirasol, Casa Costa

Orlando: It's my great pleasure to introduce two of my good friends in the industry.

Did you have any other mentors when starting out in the business?

Craig: Tom Anton Daly. He was partners with Jorge Perez from The Related Group for nearly 15 years. He never spent a day in college. He was gifted with a very intuitive mind for everything from land acquisition to understanding construction costs to completely understanding the sales and marketing process and market cycles. He mentored me on all those topics.

Orlando: What about you, Philip?

Philip: Actually, my former father-in-law brought me into the industry back in 1969. I got a tremendous education from the ground up—sales, marketing, construction, finance—and he inspired me to want to do it for the rest of my life.

Orlando: You developed the famous Miami Report. Why, and what have you learned from it?

Craig: We created the Miami Report for a very specific audience. We created it in the middle of 2009. Remember, back then it was a falling knife environment. Prices were dropping, and nobody had a sense of urgency. Everybody in sales understands that in order to sell, you need to create a sense of urgency.

Philip and I had a problem: We had to pay the rent, and we had to make payroll. We needed commission income. How would we start getting the commission income going again when there was zero feeling of urgency out there? We had to give the sales people a reason to feel the urgency.

We were in the middle of a worldwide financial crisis in every sector of the economy, so how was it that the condos in Miami were going to come out of this okay or better than ever?

We decided to go out there and find out just how bad it was. My late father used to say, "The dark clouds in your life are usually much farther away than they appear." We decided to count, literally, how many condos were really for sale in Miami, so we went out, building by building. We were able to give our sales people a real count of what was out there.

There were 10,000 units, and most agents' estimates were way off, by about 150%. By a year later, in the summer of 2010, that number was down to around 7,500 units, and dropping fast.

The Miami Report gets into the reasons for why that was going on. Our sales people went from feeling like they were walking into a funeral home to feeling like they had won lottery tickets simply because we gave them information.

Orlando: Knowledge.

Craig: Information is knowledge.

Our sales people would say, "Can we share this with our brokers?" We agreed, if they would translate it into Spanish and Portuguese.

Next, we thought we could use these ourselves as a listing to offer to developers to consider ISG. It worked! The next thing we knew, we were publishing the ISG Miami Report twice a year, every year.

It tells the story of where we are.

Orlando: You've been in real estate for many years. I want to hear about a failure or a tough time that you went through and what you learned from it.

Philip: Back in 2000, we were starting to get ourselves established when 9/11 happened. As for so many people, it became a very challenging time for us.

Orlando: What did you learn from that experience?

Philip: Never give up. The tougher things became for us, the harder we put our noses to the grindstone and worked harder. We went out and told our story to enough people, and we started getting new business and diversifying.

That's when we started entering markets just outside of Miami. By 2002 and 2003, we were in control of over 20,000 apartments and condos to sell, conversions, new construction. We were doing business in Las Vegas, Puerto Rico, and Panama.

Our game plan, which had been very difficult when things were slow and we were transitioning, actually started to come to fruition. Tough times and quick results gave us the fortitude to get through what we went through in 2008, 2009, and 2010.

Orlando: Both of you deal with a lot of real estate agents on a daily basis. What are the common problems you see? What advice would you give to those agents?

Craig: For me, it's information. If you're going to compete at a high level, you need to be informed.

Philip: We're selling high-price, luxury real estate to very sophisticated people, who can afford to spend $2 million, $4 million, and $10 million. They aren't coming to the table without some knowledge of what's going on. They know if you are giving them bad information or if you're just not knowledgeable. If you want to compete, and you want to be able deal with people at that level, you have to be prepared.

You can get a real estate license without a lot of time or effort, but you can't make money at it without putting in the time, the effort, and the commitment to know your business. That's a good rule of thumb for any business, but in our industry it's absolutely critical. It's not good enough to be well-dressed and good-looking; you have to know what you're talking about.

Orlando: What's the best real estate business advice you ever received?

Craig: I got some from my mentor, Tom Daly: Truly know your competition.

If you work for Tom Daly, selling a building, he wants you to know the details of the surrounding competitive buildings. How many apartments are in each building? How large are they? What are they selling for? What is the brand of the kitchen cabinets in each building? You should know about the appliances, plumbing fixtures in the bathrooms, and how many parking spots there are per unit.

The details Tom wanted you to know about the competition were extraordinary but very helpful because if you knew when a customer walked into your office, you were totally confident that you could handle the client's questions. The customer would take you seriously and trust you. Customers are about to spend a lot of money with you, so they need to know that they're doing business with a person with strong values, not just somebody who's attractive.

For example, Tom Daly and Jorge Perez, the biggest developer in Florida, is very intense. When you work with him, you have to bring your A-game. If you're not prepared to get into a conversation, you would never do so with Tom Daly, and you certainly shouldn't with Jorge Perez.

Orlando: What about Donald Trump? You've also worked with him in the past year?

Craig: Donald Trump is a genius promoter. Philip and I never got the chance to work with him as closely as we did with guys like Tom Daly and Jorge Perez, in terms of getting into the nitty gritty details. Nonetheless, when it comes to promoting himself as a brand, Donald Trump is a genius.

Orlando: How do you maintain your A-game and your focus in this fast-paced environment?

Craig: You have to find time to unhook. What we've learned teaches us that the human brain doesn't really move into creative mode until it stops responding. If you don't find time to turn off these damn electronic devices, then you have a problem.

Orlando: How do you do it?

Craig: My wife is a crazy athlete from Brazil, and she has me in the gym every morning at 7:00, doing something. When you're exercising, you have to think about what you're doing, so I am not thinking about management, emails, or text messages. It helps me.

When I'm finished, I start thinking about my sales presentations because sales presentations are very creative.

Orlando: Can you elaborate on how you approach sales presentations? I think it's genius.

Craig: I teach everyone in my sales team that every presentation has two connections: the logical connection and the emotional connection.

The audience has to like what they are buying. No one ever bought a house that they didn't like. In fact, they need to love it. You have to create both connections at the same time, the logical connection and the emotional connection. You're not going to sell a home, whether it's a condo or a house, without making both connections.

Orlando: If you could recommend one daily practice to real estate agents to succeed in this business, what would it be?

Philip: Knowledge.

Craig: After knowledge comes investment. Successful agents pay for their own assistance. They understand the value of a support team. You can't do it all yourself.

If you hire an assistant who understands how important it is to help you network and then follow up, you can do what you do best, which is usually making presentations. If you do three or four presentations a day, you're done; you have no energy left. You need somebody else to do the other stuff.

Orlando: If you could recommend one action for real estate agents today, whether they are new or experienced, what action would that be?

Philip: If you can't hear a "No," you shouldn't be in this business. There are so many "No's" before you hear a "Yes," and you have to be able to pump yourself up and be willing to go out and make the next call.

Also, don't accept what you hear. Don't even accept what you read in the newspaper. Go and learn the market. Go see the projects. Get to understand them yourself, and don't take other people's preconceived concepts.

Interview #4: Chris Leavitt

Chris Leavitt, not only a top producer in Miami but also in New York and West Palm Beach, you've seen him on Fox Business, *The Street with Maria Bartiromo*, and, of course, the *One Million Dollar Listing*. In 2015 he closed over $100 million in sales.

Orlando: How long have you been in the business of real estate, and why did you choose real estate?

Chris: I've been in the real estate business for about 20 years. I started the day after I graduated college.

I wanted to be a businessman, and I was told by someone very smart that at one point in your life, you have to live in New York City. It's like graduate school for just growing up.

I moved to New York and immediately interviewed with the Corcoran Group and Douglas Elliman. I chose Corcoran because it was near my apartment. They are both great companies. I am with Douglas Elliman now but chose Corcoran at the time, and within three weeks, I had a listing for $3.5 million.

Orlando: What did you do during the first three weeks to get those listings?

Chris: Back in the day, there were for-sale-by-owners, but they were called "open listings." The market was good in the mid-90s, so people were busy and unfocused. I got started mailing to the buildings and doing the old-school stuff that we do as agents.

My business grew, and then I partnered with somebody who had a big listing on Central Park West. I got a lot of business from that, and my business sky-rocketed.

Then, in 2001, I had my best summer. I was about to get $1 million in commissions when September 11th happened, and I lost every single deal. That was my first wake-up call in real estate to save my money. Don't spend your money until that check has cleared the bank.

That experience really matured me in the industry and also taught me how to ride those waves, the ups and the downs in our market.

Orlando: Did you have a mentor during the early years?

Chris: Yes, when I was 17 years old and in high school, we were given a senior project. In the last six weeks of school, we were given the opportunity to do whatever we wanted to do or go anywhere to intern with somebody in an industry that we thought we wanted to get into.

I flew down to Palm Beach because it was February in Boston and still cold. I interned with Lawrence Moens, the number-one agent in Palm Beach. Lawrence has his own company. He has a flip-phone, and he doesn't have email. He's old-school, but he makes millions of dollars a year.

I interned with him and followed him for six weeks. I saw how he makes so much money without working all that much; however, when he worked, it was smart, not hard. I learned the philosophy, "Work smart, not hard." That's how Lawrence Moens got the job done. He has incredible time-management ability. He mentored me to live that way because I wanted to enjoy my life, live lavishly, and not be bugged down 24/7 doing ridiculous things. A lot of agents go into the office, work for 10 hours, and don't get many things done.

Orlando: "Don't confuse activity with productivity." You are close to selling over $100 million this year. One hundred million dollars in sales is a lot of real estate. Certainly, you are not working 10 times more than the person who sells $10 million a year. Clearly, that's about working smart.

What are some of things that you do to work smart, rather than harder? What advice would you give to an agent?

Chris: As an agent, you need to be the industry expert. You need to be the authority on not just real estate but everything to do with business finance. Don't let your client tell you something about the sale that just happened. You need to read *The Wall Street Journal* and *The New York Times*. I have Google alerts for Aspen, Beverly Hills, London, and China real estate. I read every morning about all of the markets because you don't know who you're dealing with and where they're coming from.

Miami is a global city; people come from all over the world, so you need to know your audience. When I moved to Miami, I took culture courses because I wanted to learn all about the different cultures.

Orlando: What habits have you developed to acquire that knowledge that converts into confidence?

Chris: Uber. I live in Palm Beach predominantly. I have an apartment in Miami, but I spend so much time on I-95 and didn't want to waste that time.

Don't text and drive, and don't email. No text is worth your life. I love my car so much, I love driving it, and I don't want to destroy it. I love my life as well.

Take Uber, or invest in a driver, so whenever you have to be in the car, you're maximizing your time. Don't waste a minute driving, and you will have a lot of time.

Orlando: What attributes make the most successful real estate agent? What has made you so successful in real estate?

Chris: I think being extremely knowledgeable makes someone successful. The media helps too. Being on Fox Business news, Bloomberg, and shows like *Million Dollar Listing* was fun, but I think it also helped me in my business because it elevated me to the level of expert.

Social media is really important as well. I have a publicist. Even if you're not famous, you may want to invest in somebody to help boost your image.

Orlando: You're famous at a national level, but other agents can be famous in their communities. That is more than enough to make a very good living.

Chris: If you love Bay Harbor Islands, be Mr. Bay Harbor, and invest your money in your marketing. Consider hiring a publicity team to elevate you to the level of expert. Make sure you're in Bay Harbor magazine, if that exists. Make sure that you're the agent to go to.

Orlando: You work in New York, Palm Beach, and Miami. What is your biggest sale in Miami?

Chris: I held the record for a year at $34 million but just got trumped by a $60 million sale at the famous new building Faena.

Orlando: What did you learn in New York that made you so competitive and gave you the advantage in South Florida? How do you compare the New York business environment to Miami? Does that give you an edge?

Chris: Absolutely. New York has such a fast pace. There's no time or space for complacency. I think in Miami people show up a little bit later. In New York City you cannot be two minutes late; there's no tolerance for that.

Orlando: That makes your business easier in Miami; you can dominate much easier there than in New York.

Chris: Yes, absolutely. I feel like I could outwork 90% of some agents.

Orlando: What advice would you give to a new agent or to an experienced agent?

Chris: If you want to grow your business, you should notify everyone that you know that you're in the real estate business. You can do that with an announcement card or an email, and you should utilize social media because it's free. I've sold apartments on social media, through Facebook, Instagram, and Twitter. It works. It's a useful tool, but do it right, manage it right, and separate your personal life from your business.

Interview #5: Darin Tansey

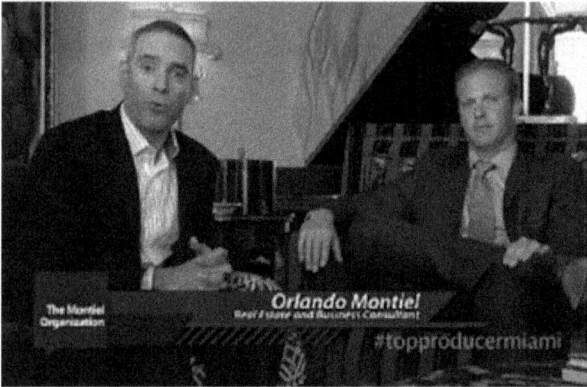

Darin Tansey works with Douglas Elliman and has one of the strongest team in the company, currently with over $125 million in listings in South Florida and over $75 million worldwide.

Orlando: Darin closed about $55 million in sales for 2014.

What's your background? How long have you been in the business, and how did you get started in real estate?

Darin: I was born and raised in Iowa. I went to school at Western Illinois University and majored in Communications and Business Management Psychology.

After that, I moved to Chicago, where I lived for eight years. I started at Johnson & Johnson. I've been selling for over 20 years.

My first professional sales job was as a pharmaceutical sales rep. I called on psychiatrist neurologist when the ADHD medication first came out. That's really how I got started in sales.

In terms of real estate, I once sold three of my own properties in Chicago. On the first one I made $65,000. I thought to myself, "I just made $65,000 more than what I paid for this? I might be on to something."

That piqued my interest. I bought and sold a couple more, and, at 30, I made a life transition from Chicago to South Florida, where I've been for almost nine years.

Orlando: I want to ask you about your sales training at Johnson & Johnson. What most people lack in real estate is the sales training. How was it in the company?

Darin: My corporate training at Johnson & Johnson was pivotal to my success. I learned how to work and become a professional. I learned to prepare yourself and how the sales process works. It's a very long process, and it comes with relational building.

Training is also about the foundation of selling and Selling 101 skills, which many people lack in real estate. They forget that this is a sales job. You're selling yourself; you're selling a product; you're selling an area; and you're selling an idea, a concept, and a lifestyle. A lot of people forget that.

Orlando: I came from the financial industry, first with Nations Bank and then Bank of America, which both had very structured and formal sales training. They taught you how to find clients, prequalify them, follow up. They made sure you understood how to make a presentation and the objections, then finally how to close them and build a relationship for life.

That's something we need to learn in real estate. Most agents don't have that training. They don't have a system to follow up, and even fewer have a formal presentation. They don't even know how many objections there are.

I ask many agents, "How many objections are there?"

They say, "There are many."

As a matter of fact, there are only eight objections. If you learn the answers to those objections, your chances of closing the client increase tremendously.

Did you have any mentors at the beginning of your professional career?

Darin: I have a professional mentor, Jay Parker, the CEO of Douglas Elliman. Jay and I have known each other for close to seven years, and I look at how Jay presents himself both personally and professionally in his life.

Orlando: Can you share with us one failure you experienced and what you learned from it?

Darin: Moving down to Florida after I left Johnson & Johnson was both the biggest success of my life and the biggest failure.

Orlando: Why is that?

Darin: I was riding clouds, living a very comfortable life. I was very successful in the company. They wanted me to travel all around the country, open different divisions, and become a manager.

I chose to take a big risk in my life. I came down to Florida and still felt that I was riding on that cloud. At that same time, we had this small thing happen called the recession. In 2007, I got my real estate license, and I thought I would conquer the real estate world in South Florida.

Then the recession hit. I had this license in my hand, and I had no idea what to do. I hardly knew where I was going in South Florida. Nobody was buying anything.

At a point like that, you really need to go back to your core values. How do you sell? How do you find clients? I failed several times. I coined the phrase that I share with some of my close friends: "The more dirt you eat, the better the champagne tastes."

Orlando: What specific lessons did you learn from that experience?

Darin: No matter how much money you are making, whether the market is strong or the market is soft, this business is very challenging. People believe that real estate agents work 10 hours a week, make $500,000 a year, and do nothing. You work 10 hours, and then you take a lunch each day.

The truth is, the amount of money you make is equal to the amount of effort and time that you put into it. You could get lucky; there are people who get lucky, but it is difficult to be lucky consistently. I learned that you can't take anything for granted.

Orlando: Do you have any success stories that stand out?

Darin: I went to my mentor Jay Parker back in 2009 and said to him, "I don't know what to do. I'm doing all of these things, but I can't get any business."

He took a chance on me and gave me 10 listings in a rental building called Treasures on the Bay. I worked nonstop on $1,100 to $1,800 rentals like they were $18-million listings on the water.

I look at that as a success story. As simple as it sounds, I worked each and every day as hard as I could to rent those units. I learned to treat every deal as the biggest deal of my life. I'll never forget that lesson.

Orlando: Do you have a habit that allows you to perform better and become more successful?

Darin: I like to be simple. You have to be happy with what you do and with who are. Surround yourself with people who can make you better and stronger. The most important thing is to hire a good assistant.

Orlando: Great, great, point: Hire a good assistant. An assistant will pay for herself or himself many times over every month. That's one of the best investments you will ever make in your life and in your business.

Darin: We are bombarded on a daily basis, fortunately, with phone calls, texts, emails, meetings, and deadlines. It's non-stop, all day long. If I don't have a support team, I can't have a life.

You need to be able to delegate responsibilities. You need to have your own time and family time. You need to be a smart professional. You can't do everything. You need to learn how to balance the stress that comes with this position, which is non-stop every single day.

Orlando: Struggling agents see paying for an assistance as an expense, right?

Darin: That's right; it's an expense to them.

Orlando: Top agents see paying for an assistant as an investment.

Darin: It is an investment. You need to spend money to make money.

Orlando: Do you have a daily habit that contributes to your success?

Darin: Good time management is key. It's as simple as it sounds.

Time is our most valuable asset. Whether you're in real estate or you're a doctor or a lawyer, time is your most valuable asset. If you are able to channel that time and really understand what you want to achieve each and every day with a good assistant, you will be able to find success.

Orlando: Do you use any tools to manage your activities and time?

Darin: My tool is my alarm clock on my phone. It wakes me up at 6 AM and gets me to the gym by 6:45. The morning is the most important time. I use that not only as a stress-reliever but for health and as a time to focus and really think about what my goals are for the day. That's the time for myself when I can visualize the things I need to prioritize.

Orlando: There's a saying that goes, "You either tell your day where to go, or at the end of the day, you will ask yourself where it went."

Darin: You have to stop and think about what you do as a professional each and every day. What do you want to achieve? Where do you want to be in one year? Where do you see yourself in 10 years, and how are you going to achieve that? You can't just think about what you are going to do tomorrow. You need to have a plan.

Orlando: If you could give one piece of advice to an agent who is just getting started in the business, what would it be?

Darin: I get asked that question a lot. I use the same analogy each and every time. I tell new agents, "Visualize a triangle. Now flip it up upside-down. On top of the base of that triangle, are the words 'real estate'.

"Real estate is like a tree: There are different branches that represent residential, commercial, etc. You have to really think and get to the point. What do you know? What do you like? What are you passionate about? What do you see yourself doing day in and day out, and where can you make yourself an expert versus the rest of your competition?"

Orlando: If you could give a piece of advice to an experienced agent, what would it be?

Darin: Even if you're the top producer in your company and made $5 million, don't get complacent with yourself. Don't get complacent with your goals, and don't get complacent with your level of success.

Interview #6: Jay Parker

Jay Parker, Chief Executive Officer of Douglas Elliman Real Estate's Florida Brokerage

Jay began his career at the Law Firm of Gunster Yoakley Valdez Fauli & Stewart in both the Miami and Palm Beach Real Estate Departments. In his first years as an attorney, Parker was fundamental to one of the firms client's international rollout handling over $300mm in mergers and acquisitions, finally leading the client to an IPO. In 2000, Parker moved to New York City where he was General Counsel for LandTel Communications.

In late 2001, Jay moved back to Miami Beach from New York City to form Clear Title Group and was quickly able to distinguish the it as one of the largest and most successful real estate law firms in Miami Beach, representing many of Miami Beach's most respected developers, landlords, tenants and handling some of the most significant real estate transactions. Today, he is the CEO of Douglas Elliman Florida Brokerage.

Orlando: Jay, tell me about your background. How did you get started in the real estate industry?

Jay: Real estate has been in my blood since I was born. I grew up in a family of real estate. My father is a real estate lawyer, and my mother was a real estate agent.

I moved to Florida in 1993 for law school. During law school, I started working for real estate developers both in Miami and in Palm Beach. After graduating from law school I worked in a real state division of a large local law firm, and then ultimately I started my own law firm and title insurance company, having a passion for real estate and really loving deals.

I love to work with REALTORS® and be a dealmaker. I was fortunate enough to work with some of the most exciting and powerful entrepreneurs and REALTORS® in Miami and the Miami Beach area.

I have been in real estate for more than 20 years now and recently had the opportunity to meet with Howard Lorber, the chairman of our company. He persuaded me to take the next move in my career and take the helm of Douglas Elliman in Florida to help to make it the powerhouse that it is in New York and Florida.

Orlando: In what way?

Jay: With a higher level of professionalism and higher expectations—the bar has been raised. As real estate professionals, it's sexy to talk about luxury, new buildings, new projects, and new hotels. All of that breeds the demand for a higher level in every area of our industry—service, quality of restaurants, hotels, hospitals, schools. Every aspect of our market has been challenged to raise the bar. Clients are looking for data and professionalism.

Orlando: Did you have a mentor growing up in your career?

Jay: I have had a couple of mentors. When I was practicing law, I worked with a gentleman named Jerry Erin, who was the first senior partner that I worked with. He helped me to navigate important decisions, getting me directions, not only in business but also in my personal life. I respect him for his family and for his commitment to his family.

As my life has evolved, I have been fortunate enough to align with another mentor, a gentleman named David Bloom, who built one of the largest shopping center companies in the country.

Orlando: What did you learn from him?

Jay: He has taught me how to build businesses and how to create a corporate culture. One of the most important criteria for people today when looking for jobs is corporate culture. Corporate culture has become almost more important to many people than salaries and income.

I also learned from my Chairman, Howard Lorber, about the importance of planning and how to manage expectations. He is an extremely intelligent man that has built many successful businesses. He said to me from the very first time we met that he knows it's going to take time for me to execute on this and to not get consumed with having to be successful quickly but instead to build this right.

Orlando: You talk about the importance of differentiating yourself. Can you elaborate on that?

Jay: It's important to understand that in order to have success in this business, the first question you have to ask yourself is, "How am I going to differentiate myself from the other 37,000 agents in South Florida alone? What is my powerful message, and what's the value that I bring to the table?"

Very few take the time to ask those questions, and even fewer take the time to develop a powerful message and practice delivering that message to their clients.

We have become a much more sophisticated society; people look for what distinguishes you. Certainly, we have a number of very, very significant powerful real estate professionals in this market. I take my hat off to them, and I admire their success, but I think that as we grow and the market becomes bigger, stronger, more expensive, and more diverse, distinguishing yourself is something that you must learn to do. Most agents don't know how. Teaching and working with an agent at Douglas Elliman to help them identify distinguishing characteristics, like how they are going to market a property, just separates us from the rest.

The bars are being raised in all areas. New York buyers are not coming down to South Florida and purchasing $10 million apartments with somebody who can't get good information. They are going to ask about all kinds of things, and you need to know the answers to those questions. Any REALTOR® who doesn't understand the economics behind their market is failing themselves. Too many agents fly by the seat of their pants. They get up in the morning, go into the office, and think about what they're going to do, but they don't have a plan.

As real estate professionals, it's incumbent upon us to enhance our knowledge all the time through education. Once we have our education, it's through implementation that we achieve success. For example, so many postcards come to me, and I speak to all of the agents out there. Pay attention to the mail that you send. Take a look at what the finished product is, and if it doesn't represent professionalism and perfection, don't waste your money. I have seen mailers come to my house with the agent's picture cut off, spelling mistakes in the language, and just a picture of a sale. What do I care about the home you just sold last month?

Orlando: You touch on two very important points. Number one is the planning. We go through four steps in the program. First, we need to plan, but after the plan we need to prepare for that plan. Then you need to execute on that plan you just talked about, and then you need to review the plan so that you can improve it. You just said it.

Talk to me a bit about the importance of building relationships and having a plan.

Jay: To me, a tenant is a buyer, and a landlord is a seller. If you have the opportunity to build a relationship with them, do it. It will benefit your business in the long run. Contact that tenant after six months, and ask them how they like their property. Contact them at month 10, and ask them if they are going to look for something else or if they want to stay there. First of all, you are preserving your ability to earn a commission again, and second of all, you are building a relationship.

You create a business plan for 2016, but you're not going to use the same plan for 2017.

If you are going to build a business, build it from the ground up. Start with rentals. Learn how to sell $100,000, $200,000, $300,000, and $500,000 apartments. Do a little bit of the work to try to get to the bigger, more expensive residential communities, and with time, patience, and persistence, you'll get there. Everyone wants that big deal.

Orlando: It's a process.

Jay: The sophisticated agent asks himself after getting a big commission, "How much of it am I going to allocate to marketing and branding?"

Orlando: If you were to give a piece of advice to a new agent, what would it be?

Jay: Join a real estate brokerage firm where you are going to learn the basics. Don't try to reach for the stars; learn what you have to do, learn about your markets, pick a market that you are familiar with, and study it so you know it like the back of your hand. You cannot be a success in this industry if you don't know what you are talking about. It takes time to learn. You must understand that it takes about 12 months, full-time, to start to get traction in this business. It's the same with every business that you get into. It takes time to grow.

I tell people that you shouldn't be going into this business if you can't afford to be in it. It's a commission-based business. Save your money. Save up enough money that you have a cushion, so you are not acting out of desperation or fear, but instead you're acting with a plan that you are able to execute on.

We try to help people execute when they follow a plan, but they have to be prepared to take that risk and invest in themselves.

Orlando: Do you have a daily habit, an exercise, or a routine that has helped you become as successful as you are?

Jay: I believe that fitness is a very important part of my life. I work out every day, early in the morning. I don't bring my cellphone in with me, and I don't have my headset on. This gives me a chance to be by myself, to have my hour to get my head organized. Like I said, I don't look at anything else; I just work out.

As my life has evolved, I have been blessed with twin boys.

Now I start my day by kissing both of my kids and my wife. Sometimes I leave before they are up. I still go into their rooms and kiss them both, and that gives me the love and the passion to drive me through the day.

I will tell you one more secret: I like to start my day with the right mindset. Every single day when I get into the car, I say out loud, "Today is going to be a great day," and I mean it.

Orlando, the lessons that you're teaching the REALTORS® is a very basic recipe for success. In fact, I tell so many young people that I meet today to become REALTORS®. It's a great business.

Orlando: Thank you, Jay. What is one piece of advice for an experienced agent?

Jay: Create a business plan. Successful agents need to also spend time focusing on how to get better, bigger, and stronger. Just because you're successful doesn't mean that you can't be more successful, and it doesn't mean that you can't learn from other people. Therefore, my number-one recommendation to successful agents is to take the time to create a specific business plan of exactly how they are going to execute. At the end of that period, whether it's a year, six months, or a quarter, they should review it and figure out what worked and what didn't work.

Interview #7: Jeff Morr

Jeff Morr is a seasoned Miami real estate veteran with over 30 years in the business. He is the chairman of the Miami Master Broker's Forum, an organization comprised of the top 250 Realtors in Miami-Dade County. Jeff ventured into the real estate world at the age of 21, bringing an education in Advertising and Marketing. He introduced the "modern loft" concept in the late 1990's and took a strong part in reshaping the Miami skyline.

In 1995, Jeff Morr founded Majestic Properties, a full-service real estate organization company with strong presence throughout Miami Beach and Downtown Miami. Majestic achieved over $5 billion in sales since inception and was named fastest-growing, privately-held, full-service U.S. real estate company by INC. 500 Magazine.

In June of 2014, after two solid decades, Morr chose to relinquish his management responsibilities, as a result, Majestic Properties was sold to Douglas Elliman in June of 2014 in order for

Morr to continue to building his real estate practice in South Florida.

Orlando: Today, I have the pleasure to have with me Jeff Morr. He is one of the few agents who has been able to not only build a great real estate company but also to sell it.

What is your background, Jeff, in terms of real estate and in terms of business?

Jeff: In terms of business, I was doing everything before real estate, from mowing lawns to babysitting and selling clothing at the flea market. I was doing all kinds of things before college.

I started in real estate when I was 21, while I was studying advertising. I had a client who wanted to buy a house in Coral Springs, Florida, which I had never been to. We didn't have iPhone maps in those days, back in 1984.

I showed my client four houses, and she liked one. We went back to the office; my broker helped me write the contract; I presented it to a very, very intimidating woman in her 60s; and I put a deal together. That was equal to about three months of pay at my part-time job.

I went into real estate full-time while still going to school, and within two years, I became a partner in the company. We built it into a pretty large franchise in South Florida.

I have been doing it for a long time now, almost two-thirds of my life.

Orlando: Did you have a mentor at the time?

Jeff: No, but someone in the office told me about a course—I think it was a 13-week seminar—with Floyd Wickman. Floyd taught me how to farm, how to communicate with clients, and how to build relationships and a database. That helped me a lot. I highly recommend to every new agent to take as many courses as they can and really get themselves to the next level early on; otherwise, they won't be in the business for long.

Orlando: I'm sure, as a business owner, you have faced some challenges and some failures in the past. Do you remember a difficult situation in your business and what you learned from it?

Jeff: Recessionary times are always tricky. 2005 was not a great year for real estate in South Florida. During that time, I bumped up my marketing and ended up doing better than I have ever done before.

Orlando: Talk to me about the marketing. What do you mean when you say, "...I bumped up my marketing...?"

Jeff: That means more marketing. In those days, we didn't have social media, and we didn't have e-fliers and e-blasts. I invested a lot more money in marketing. Marketing is the key to longevity in this business.

Orlando: I want to stay on that topic because when I am doing my coaching seminars or programs, I say that we are not in the business of real estate. If we want to make above-average incomes in real estate, we need to understand that we are not in the business of real estate; we are in the business of marketing.

Can you share with me a little bit about how important marketing is or has been for your business?

Jeff: I tell agents that your broker is your mall. It's an analogy that works very well. The broker is going to give you a space in the mall, and you are going to open up your store. Every one of us, whether we own a real estate company or we work under a real estate company, we are a real estate company; we are a brand.

If you offer the best service, do a lot of marketing in the right places, and spend your money wisely, you'll be successful. The beautiful thing about real estate is that you don't even have to buy it and put it on your shelves. You don't have to stock inventory, and you have billions of dollars of it. Even so, a lot of agents don't know the market or are afraid to spend money on marketing.

Orlando: Invest!

Jeff: It's 100% investment.

Orlando: Brokers and agents see marketing as an expense. Top producers like you see it as an investment.

Jeff: Top producers are not cheap. Top producers understand the value of spending money to make money. I tell agents, "Spend $1, and you should get $10 back. You want to make $1 million? Spend $100,000 on marketing. You want to make $5 million? Spend $500,000 in marketing. When you're starting out, spend a $1,000 a month on marketing. That will give you a $120,000 a year."

This is the opposite of what someone would tend to do naturally. I understood that there is a certain amount of business out there for the grabbing and that if I increased my marketing, I would be successful. I spent $500 a month. My business exploded. People would stop me for my autograph. I understood the value of spending money.

Orlando: That's the whole point, being consistent. Most agents send a piece of marketing, and if it doesn't work within the first trial, they don't do it anymore and say it doesn't work.

Jeff: They are just throwing away their money. If you are going to do anything, commit for a year, at least. If it doesn't work after a year, then try something else.

Orlando: What are the common problems that you see real estate agents facing today?

Jeff: Number one is competition. There are too many real estate agents. It's too easy to get a real estate license. There is no guidance. Many go to small companies, where they get absolutely nothing, which is a mistake, in my opinion, for a new agent or a seasoned agent.

Orlando: What would you recommend to a new agent?

Jeff: Go to a company that has a presence and has a broker onsite that offers administrative and marketing support. Otherwise, you are wasting your time.

You want to go to a presentation with power. When you go on a listing appointment, and you come in with Joe Shmoe Realty, the company no one has ever heard of, you probably already lost that listing. You want to go in with fireworks, confidence, support, and guidance. If you need somebody to go with you on a listing appointment, you have it in a real company. Don't waste your time with a Mickey Mouse company. Go to a real company that has all the support you need, and stay with that company. Don't move around.

A lot of agents jump around for absolutely no reason. It's not the company, it's you. If you're not making it, it's you. Don't blame your broker. It's not going to be better somewhere else.

Orlando: What do you think are the common traits an agent has to have to be successful in 2014?

Jeff: It's hard work. People get in to this business thinking they will have all these flexible hours. Successful REALTORS® work hard. Work smart, qualify your sellers and market, build your business, and invest in your brand. I recommend that 20% of your income go back to your marketing.

Orlando: Can you share a success story with us and what you learned from that success?

Jeff: I have been doing this for a long time, so there are a lot of success stories, but I pride myself on breaking records. I really investigate the market, do my research, understand the value of my listing, and stand behind it. I don't take listings that are overpriced, and I leave about 5% for negotiation. If you price the property right, it's going to sell. If you price it too high to test the market, you are going to fail.

They say that the third agent is the one that gets lucky. I don't want to be the third agent. I want to be the first agent and make it happen, so I have a lot of success stories to do with pricing aggressively, not below market but just above market, leaving myself a little room to negotiate. People like to negotiate, and that's how you put money in your pocket. Price it right, sell it quickly; get it done, and break a record.

Orlando: When you say "break a record," can you name one of the records that you have broken?

Jeff: Seventy-million-dollar hotel. I've sold 600 units in a condo in one day.

Orlando: In terms of your real estate business, what's the best advice you have ever received?

Jeff: I tend to give more advice than I receive because I have been doing it for so long. The best advice that I give my agents who want to start real estate companies is, DON'T.

Orlando: Why?

Jeff: Today, it's a big boys' game. The Company that I sold to is a big, multi-billion-dollar organization. They have the tools, staying power, reach, database, and ability to market. If you are thinking about opening a real estate company with the splits being as high as they are today, don't. Go with a great broker, and make money.

Orlando: Do you have a habit that contributes to your success?

Jeff: Staying in touch with clients.

Orlando: How do you do it?

Jeff: My database receives a couple of e-fliers a week from me, including market updates, new projects, new listings, and new sales that we have just made. I don't overdo it, but a couple of times a week is okay.

I do a lot of direct mail because I believe in it. People need to see you, so staying in touch and cultivating referrals and future business is super important.

You need to be out there. I am a full-time social media person. I understand that costs money, but it's an investment. I am not telling agents to start out spending $10,000 or $20,000 a month. Spend something thought, and always invest 20% back into marketing. Build it up. Make sure that your two is better than your one and your three is better than your two, and recessions won't matter because when times are not good, sellers have to entrust their listings to the best REALTORS®. Ten percent of the people make 90% of the money in this business. If you're not going to be in the 10%, don't be in the business. The beauty of this business is that you can be 70 and 80 years old and still do it.

Orlando: You built a company, and you sold it. What key elements must a business owner have to create a successful real estate practice?

Jeff: First of all, to be a successful business owner, you need to know how to delegate. You can't do everything. You need to train people how to do their jobs and then trust them to do their jobs. If they can't do their jobs, you need to replace them with people who can, but you need to be able to share the responsibilities, or you'll explode. That's a very, very big factor in running the business.

I have somebody who handles the website. I have somebody who handles the website leads, and I have somebody who handles the e-fliers. I have a couple of people who handle the showings. Some people handle the contract work and follow-up.

Delegate, and the job gets done. If everybody knows their job, the job gets done.

Orlando: Having a system is what we teach in coaching. If you don't have a system and you need to be present in your workplace, you don't have a business; you just have a job.

Jeff: Correct. I don't sit at a desk. I'm in restaurants and conference rooms. My office is my iPhone. Learn to let go. Trust the people that you work with. If they are not the right people, change them, but don't try to be a control freak and do everything because you'll fail.

Also, sometimes they have ideas that you don't, so have regular meetings. We meet weekly to discuss ideas, and then we implement those ideas.

Orlando: Do you have a routine to release stress?

Jeff: First of all, I exercise. I work out, run, do yoga, and take vacations. I know agents who don't take vacations, which is crazy. You should be spending a couple of months a year on vacations. Get away. Get outside of your life. Look inside your life from the outside. You'll learn new things, and you'll come up with fresh ideas from different places. Take a break, and find balance. If you're not balanced and you're working all the time, you're going to be miserable and have a heart attack.

Orlando: If you could give one piece of advice to a new agent and to an experienced agent, what would it be?

Jeff: Don't be cheap.

It takes money to make money. Invest money back into marketing. Learn, study, and network. Build relationships, and invest in those relationships. Take your clients to dinner sometimes. Send out branded gifts like pens, t-shirts, or baseball caps— anything you can do to get your clients to think of you. Obviously, be in touch with them via database, e-blasts, direct mail, and magazine advertising. You can't just do one thing. Consistency is a must.

Interview #8: John Sandberg

John Sandberg from the Sandberg Nortmann Group, with Douglas Elliman Real Estate.

Based in Miami, Florida, the Sandberg Nortmann Group is one of South Florida's premier luxury real estate team, having represented more than $100 million in 2014 and 2015. Together, John Sandberg and Ann Nortmann have 17 years experience in Miami's luxury real estate market and have successfully sold out several major projects in record time.

The Sandberg Nortmann Group specializes in marketing and selling the most exclusive, boutique-style developments, condominiums and residential real estate in downtown Miami, Miami and the Beaches, and for their efforts both have been recognized with Top Producer honors in 2014, 2013 and 2011 and are consistently in the Top 2 percent of realtors in the Southeast United States.

Orlando: What's your background, and how did you get started in real estate?

John: I'm from Boston, but I went to college in Dallas, Texas and majored in Finance.

I worked at Bear Stearns, where I was a managing director for 13 years. Before that, I worked at another firm that's no longer around, so I was in the finance world for 18 to 20 years.

Orlando: You have the most expensive listing in downtown Miami right now: $21.95 million, over 60 properties for sale. Last year your team production was over $100 million in sales. I want to go back to where you got started, where you are now, and how long it took you to get there.

John: I got my license in September 2006. The market had slowed down, and some people were becoming extremely negative, but nobody foresaw what was going to happen between 2007 and 2010. I certainly didn't. I had a tough year in 2008, but I was not alone. It was a very tough time.

Orlando: What did you learn from that situation?

John: Anything can happen. I remember being on Wall Street on a Tuesday morning, September 11. I was working at Bear Stearns. We were walking out of a morning meeting, everything was great, and life changed in an instant. I lost more money in 2008 when Bear Stearns imploded, but that was another opportunity for me to really learn about myself. I went through my victim, feel-sorry-for-me stage.

Orlando: We were talking off-camera about a very particular time in your career in real estate when you had no listings. You have over 60 listings right now, but at that time just eight years ago, you had zero listings. Explain to us what you did at that time.

John: I pulled in the small number of people that I take advice from. I read a book that really helped me called *The Millionaire Real Estate Agent*. I was already in Miami, but I'm not from there.

I don't come from a rich family, and I recognize that I'm not socially connected down here. I recognized that I could take my skills from the investing business in dealing with high-net-worth individuals and plug it in over here. That's what I embarked on when I read the book I mentioned. The premise of the book is listings, leverage, and leads—the three Ls.

Let's start with leads. You have to accumulate leads. They come from everywhere: conversations, marketing, etc. Then you need to refine your leads and build a database.

The second step is getting listings. Listings are your business. Buyers come and go, and buyers will let you down. Some of my biggest trades have been with buyers, but this is not how you build a business. You build a business with listings—listings you can manage. Listings document that you have weight and that you have a place in the business.

Finally, the book talks about bringing leverage, bringing on an assistant. The book really spoke to me, so I did the things it recommended, but at the beginning I had nothing.

Orlando: Please share with the readers your first listing.

John: In 2006, I was in the office doing floor time. I felt pretty good about myself. I'd been a managing director at this Wall Street investment banking firm, and here I was, having to be right-sized and humble, which in itself wasn't humble, if you think about it.

A nice Jamaican man walked in and said to me "I'd like to list my house. Will you come and see it?"

I agreed. I had the briefcase, the suit, the French cuffs, and the presentation. I was ready to list this thing. Not only did I want to list it, I had to list it. I had the eye on the prize.

I get to his house, and he doesn't really have anywhere for me to sit.

Orlando: Where was the house?

John: In Liberty City.

Orlando: This was one of the lowest-priced areas in the city. It's not Downtown Miami, where you can have a $22 million listing.

John: I got to the listing appointment, and he didn't have a place for me to sit, so he wanted us to sit in the backyard. He took a bucket, turned it upside-down, and said, "Would you like to sit here, on a plastic bucket?"

I had the suit on, and the sun was beating on my face. I remember thinking, "This is where it all starts. This is funny. Where's the camera?"

I pitched the guy because I wanted that listing. I think he gave it to me about three days later after several phone calls, and I sold it. It all started there.

Orlando: Great lesson. Most of us start from zero, and we build our businesses one step at a time.

John: It took me a while to realize you should never give up. Particularly in this business, you can have a life-changing experience with somebody you meet. Young agents come to me all the time and ask, "How do you do this?"

I will say something like, "Work really hard. Be really focused on whatever you want to do. Do not be a jack-of-all-trades and master of none. Get really good at what you do.

"People are paying attention to you. They won't to do business with you right away, but if they respect your knowledge of the market, they respect your integrity, and they respect your hard work, you will eventually get business."

Orlando: Can you share with me one specific success story, what you learned from it, and how you apply it today in your business?

John: About a year ago, I had some nice business that I had done, but I had never done over a $4.5-million sale.

One day I walked into the office in the morning with my partner Anne Nortmann, and a connection of the chairman of our firm at Douglas Elliman wanted to have lunch with us. I had no idea who it was, but he wanted to pick our brain about a project in Sunset Harbour in Miami Beach that we had just sold out. It was 43 luxury units in one of the hottest areas in Miami Beach called Palau Sunset Harbour. We sold 43 units in 134 days. We got a lot of positive exposure, and the chairman of our company wanted a developer from New York to talk to us. He's a very big name in New York; anybody who is in the business knows who he is. He wanted to have lunch with us, and I didn't even know who it was at the time.

We had a two-hour lunch, and at the end of the lunch, he mentioned that he had a house and asked me what I thought it would sell for. I didn't have any idea that he wanted to sell it, but the next thing you know, he says goodbye.

It was a great to talk to and have lunch with a guy like that because he was so smart. I learned a lot from that. Two hours later, the chairman of our company called me.

Orlando: Let me stop you right there. What did you learn from that conversation? What's one thing that stands out when speaking to a person who is so successful in business.

John: He knows exactly what he's doing, and he is an expert in that one area. That guy I'm fascinated by does not use a computer. He's not that much older than me. He has ideas and visions, and he implements them. Everybody else in his world handles a lot of stuff like most of us, but he's polarized, which is interesting.

Orlando: Do you know that I've met and interviewed extremely successful people who don't have computers or cellphones. I still don't know how do they do it, but they are extremely productive.

John: It's amazing.

Orlando: You came out of that lunch meeting with this very successful business person, and the chairman called you. What happened next?

John: The chairman was talking to us all about development and how it really works down here in Miami versus the rest of the world. We were as frank, open, and honest as we could be. At the very end he said, "John, you do more general real estate. What would this house on this certain island sell for if it's in immaculate, perfect condition?"

I said $1,200 to $1,400 a foot, depending. I didn't expect anything to come of my answer.

Two hours later, my phone rang. It was a blocked call, and it was the chairman of our company, Mr. Howard Lorber, who called me. I had never talked to him before. Mr. Lorber told me to call him Howard, so I felt better. He said that the individual that we just met with would like me to list his house for fourteen-and-three-quarter million dollars.

I never saw that coming. It put us on a different level. I still go to many listing appointments and don't get the listings, but as we build our resume of past success stories, it's becoming better and better.

Orlando: You just mentioned something that is so important and means a lot for a top producer. You can go to many listing appointments and still won't get all the listings. By the way, there is no agent who gets all the listings to which he or she presents. You're okay with that when it happens. You put in all your effort, and you use all your tools and knowledge, but you understand that sometimes it won't happen.

That's something we are very adamant about in our coaching program. You need to make sure that you make an amazing presentation in less than 30 minutes, including the objections. It is time to leave after 30 minutes because that's when you usually start fighting and proving points.

John: It's true. I had one yesterday for an hour and a half, and I just had to end it.

Orlando: If you can't prove a point, and the other person can't see the value you're bringing to the table in 30 minutes, he won't see it in 45 minutes or an hour.

Sometimes it's not you; sometimes it's that the other person is just not ready, so make sure that you understand the process of the presentation. Of course, if it's a big house, like the 9,000-square-foot listing you have right now, it would take a little bit longer. You need to know exactly at what time you have to end that conversation.

What's the best advice you've ever received?

John: Success leaves clues. I see a lot of new agents who have all these ideas, like they're going to deal only with royal families or $10 million properties. That's fantastic, but they fail.

Successful people in our business do the major things all the same way. When we are new, we want to come up with all of these creative ideas when we don't know what we are doing. It's a recipe for disaster.

Orlando: I've interviewed so many real estate top producers like yourself, and the pattern is pretty much the same. They have a plan. We teach a four-step process in our coaching system. First, you need to plan. Second, prepare for that plan. Third, execute, and, finally, review it, so you can do it much better next time.

What advice would give an agent that is just getting started in the business?

John: It's almost predictable that everybody comes in and says they want to do $10 million houses. They try to crack it in that market, and that takes years, but I didn't realize that then. I thought it was automatic. I did so many different things, but I started to realize that I had to do one thing. What is that thing? I started with the farm of 1,200 people and just started marketing towards them. It happened to be in area where I live. I got the piece of advice from two successful agents in the firm that I was at. I took them to lunch and said, "How did you do what you were doing?"

They taught me to start with a small farm area. They taught me how to see whether there are enough transactions. In the first year, if you market the property and you get 10% of the market, you make a living. I lived in Belle Island in South Beach, and there were 1,200 names in about five or six buildings, and I just started marketing.

Orlando: What is the one piece of advice you would give an experienced agent?

John: The biggest piece of advice I would give experienced agents and which I'm trying to do myself, is to stay humble, stay true to what you're doing, and don't get too fancy just because you have a couple of big listings.

I love being associated with big listings, but I don't forget that the $700,000 property is the bread and butter that feeds my marketing and provides me with the dollars to go after bigger markets.

Keep working, stay humble, and stay right-sized. Also remember that nothing stays the same. My old manager used to say, "The only thing that's constant is change, and you better change with it." We have to change.

Orlando: I'm reading a book called The Plateau Effect with research over 50 years. The promise of the book is very simple: Everything works until it doesn't work anymore.

Fifteen years ago, I would do cold-calling. It used to work, but 15 years later, it doesn't work if you want to build a business. People are way too smart for cold-calling. We have technology that identifies who is calling. Granted, there might be a few people who are still good at it, but do you want to build your business like that? I don't think so. Things change, and you need to evolve; you need to innovate in this business.

John: Stay teachable.

Orlando: Yes, very well said. Thank you very much for coming to the show.

John: It's been my pleasure. Thank you so much.

Interview #9: Nancy Batchelor

Nancy Batchelor, Top producer for EWM Realty International and Christie's International Real Estate. The following are just a few of her professional accomplishments:

• 2014 Chairman's Club Diamond Level for $108,500,000 in Sales and Highest Number of Units Closed in Miami Beach.

• Ranked #2 Team in Miami Beach by The Wall Street Journal/Real Trends

• Named Top Ten REALTOR® by Miami Monthly and REALTOR® Association of Miami and the Beaches

• #1 Team in Miami Beach at EWM Realty International

• In the Top 50 Women-Led Business Leaders in Florida.

Orlando: I have the true pleasure to interview one of the top producers in Miami, Nancy Batchelor. This year she closed over one hundred and ten million dollars in sales and over ninety-five transactions.

Thank you for having me in your beautiful Miami Beach house. It's going to be a pleasure to talk to you on camera. We have known each other for a while, and we've worked together in coaching.

We have talked for about 45 minutes before this interview, and we have so many things to share. You're so kind to allow me in your house, and welcome to the show!

In my coaching program, one of the things that impressed me the most about you is your work ethic. It's not that you don't have to work, but you work so, so hard for your business. Why?

Nancy: Because I love it. I'm lucky to have a job I love.

Orlando: What do you love so much about real estate?

Nancy: Real estate is about people. It's about family. It's about design and architecture, and those are all things I love.

Orlando: Did you have a mentor when you got started in real estate 15 years ago?

Nancy: Ron Shuffield. He's our president at EWM. He always wears the white hat and takes the high road. He knows his numbers. He's also very much into statistics, and he's been a great teacher and a mentor for me.

Orlando: You've built one of the most successful real estate practices in Miami. What are some of the attributes that contribute to your success in business?

Nancy: There are four things. First is marketing. We are consistent with our marketing, whether it's off-season or in-season.

Second, I have a wonderful team that packs my parachute every day. They also have great sales ability, and they can each work a certain area of town. They each have qualities of their own that really help me sell.

Fourth is having the passion and the energy.

Orlando: I'm sure you have some failures, like any other successful business owner. What is one failure that you remember, and what did you learn from that failure?

Nancy: I love listing and marketing, and often I will go into listing presentations against my friends and competitors. Every time you go in there, and you don't get the listing, I think that is a bit of a failure.

In reality, however, those failures make you stronger. You analyze them and try to discuss them with the customer. Why did they pick somebody else over you? I think you can be a better agent if you take those failures, turn them around, get back on the horse, and do a better presentation next time.

Orlando: What do you do when that happens to you?

Nancy: A lot of it is practice, repetition, knowing what most of the common questions are, and being prepared. Many agents go into listing presentations and just wing it. If a basketball team or a football team just winged it, they would probably lose, so they practice their plays. They work on teamwork, and that's how they are a team, and that's how they win. Real estate needs more of this repetition and training.

Orlando: In the down market you not only kept doing your marketing but increased it. What results did you get from that?

Nancy: I doubled my numbers. There was a lot of competition, and keeping that consistency in marketing gave consumers confidence in me. In the last three years, I've almost doubled my numbers every year.

Orlando: Can you share a success story and what you learned from that experience?

Nancy: Listen to your customers.

I had a great past client who wanted something larger. He was an avid golfer, and I had heard lots of whispering about the surf club, so I suggested we go to New York and meet with the famous architect Richard Meyer so we could get his feedback and hear what was really going on. We had a great meeting because a lot of his objections were overcome, and he proceeded to buy one of the first penthouses. He got a very good value because he was one of the first ones there. He got a dream apartment.

Orlando: Another thing that you do, outside of real estate, is being very involved in the community. Can you talk a little bit about that?

Nancy: Yes, philanthropy is near and dear to my heart, and we've got a great community here. We have lots of needs, and for the last 15 years, I have been very involved on many philanthropic boards.

I have been involved with Viscaya on the board of Fair Child. I have chaired the Frost Science Museum for four years. I'm chairing the Chapman Homeless.

I meet many of the community leaders and find out what makes Miami tick, so when my customers come here, I can give them great advice about the schools and what's available to them to do, like the symphony and the ballet. I can really talk their talk. I get to know the opportunities that exist in Miami.

It's not only about the property; it's about the things around the property, including the lifestyle. That's how you can really understand exactly what they are looking for, their needs, and the trends. You can talk about the trends, what's happening, and what's next in Miami because of involvement in the community. While you are giving back, you are updated every single month about exactly what's happening all over town.

Orlando: You talk a lot about the importance of teamwork. What advice would you give an agent that is building a team?

Nancy: They have to have a work ethic. They have to realize that each has to pull his own horse. On my team each person has a certain niche, and they help out in a lot of areas. It works very well. We can help the customer more when it's not just about me, and my team is well trained.

Something that's very important is that we have a great board. That's how I met you, in fact. The classes at our board are so good that I force all my team members to go. They go to those classes, and they are so surprised by how much they get out of them. For just a couple of hours, you can go from A to Z and understand the whole process and not fumble the ball. We are fortunate to have people like you teaching at our board. For very little money you can have some of the best people in the business teaching you.

Orlando: A lot of people are surprised when they see you there. A lot of them come to me and say "Oh look, there's Nancy Batchelor." You put a lot of effort into your work and your education as well.

What advice would you give a new agent who is getting started?

Nancy: First of all, they should go to as many classes as they can. Second, if they borrow money from their mother or whomever, they should try to get a coach.

I hired you. I was 15 years in the business, and that's how I met you. This business is so competitive that it is better to have somebody from the outside who is non-emotional and can say, "This is your strength, and this is what you should do." It will give you a shortcut because for the cost of coaching or taking classes, it is a great reward.

Orlando: What advice would you give to an experienced agent?

Nancy: Remember that what worked five years ago is not going to work now. Some longtime agents rest on their laurels. Many agents don't keep up with the technology, and they try to ignore it. Technology is not going away; it's here to stay.

Orlando: I remember interviewing Alicia Cervera and her saying, "Don't ever assume that what you're doing now that has created your success is going to create your success in the next season, in the next cycle, or in the next year," which is exactly what you are talking about; what worked yesterday won't work today. What's working today won't work tomorrow. You have to keep up with the technology, information, and trends.

What type of technology have you implemented in your business, especially in your marketing?

Nancy: I've always been a marketing and advertising person. I studied it in college, and I've always liked print: magazines, direct mail, newspapers. I have now jumped on the social media bandwagon and have tried to improve our message.

There's a new group of consumers now that want to know what you are going to do for them. One of our new slogans is, "We're not number one; you are." We are implementing more things like remembering Mother's Day, not just Christmas, and doing client parties after somebody closes. I take people horseback riding. I take people to events. I try to take them to places where we can have real conversations, not just going out for lunch or coffee, but to private social clubs or in boats, where they are completely disconnected from their phones. I can really get to know them, and that's been very beneficial.

Orlando: You said, it's all about the confidence. Confidence to me is a result of preparation. I can do all the affirmations in the world: "I'm number one. I can do it! I'm the best!" If I'm not prepared, I'm not going to have that confidence.

How do you prepare yourself to be one of the top agents in Miami?

Nancy: Three things: getting up early, fitness, and product knowledge.

You have to read a lot. You've got to be a little bit ahead of it, but just reading isn't always going to get you there. You've got to see it. It's hard to sell something you've never seen. You need to get out of the chair in front of the TV and get out there because real estate isn't always about sitting in front of the computer.

Orlando: But nobody has the time anymore, right?

Nancy: You've got to make time.

Orlando: You have to go to the office.

Nancy: In my opinion a lot of REALTORS® like being at home. I like being in an office because I have my work hat on. I'm there to work, and I also gain a lot of knowledge from the other REALTORS® there about off-market opportunities. I get a little insight edge. You don't get that same edge at home.

Interview #10: Nelson Gonzalez

Top producer and Senior Vice President of EWM Realty International, Nelson Gonzalez.
Consistently, Nelson sells over $100 million a year in luxury real estate. In 2014 alone, Nelson sold over $137 million. His hard work and dedication has placed him in the top 1% of REALTORS® in the country.

Orlando: Nelson, tell me about your background.

Nelson: I was born and raised in Miami. I grew up in South Miami and then moved to the beach when I started working in real estate.

Orlando: You've been in the business for over 27 years. Did you have a mentor?

Nelson: Yes, I had a mentor by the name of Gerald Lawrence. When I started, he did a lot of luxury residential real estate. I shadowed him for about six months. I learned the business, and I felt extremely comfortable working in the high-end. I sold my first house during my first week in real estate.

Orlando: I'm sure you learned many things from that person. Can you share with us one or two things that stand out from the experience of having somebody to guide you through the beginning?

Nelson: I learned how to follow up and talk to people. It's proven that people who continue to follow up in a nice way, not in a pushy way, eventually get the business. As the saying goes, "Out of sight, out of mind."

Orlando: You touch on a very good point. When we're coaching real estate agents, the number-one principle we teach is called the 10/90 Rule, which means that less than 10% of the people with whom you will do business will actually do it within the first 90 days of the initial contact. That's where the follow-up comes in. Actually, if you look at any agent's closings, you'll see that more than 90% of all the people that the agent closed happened after 90 days and sometimes up to two years after the initial contact.

You mentioned to me earlier the importance of asking the right questions. Can you touch on that?

Nelson: You have to identify if the buyer is actually a buyer.

I can talk to somebody for 30 seconds and know exactly where they're coming from and if they're for real or not, just by asking certain questions. I sit back and I listen.

You have to be able to identify if a buyer is actually a buyer and when they're prepared to buy. That's how you use your follow-up.

Orlando: That's critical. In coaching, we say that the success in your business is determined by the quality of the conversations you have with your clients. The quality of those conversations comes from the questions you ask, but many agents are afraid to ask.

Nelson: Absolutely. A lot of people are afraid to ask certain questions. I have found over the years that many high-end buyers want you to take them by the hand and guide them, telling them what they should buy. By asking the right questions, you really understand where they are coming from.

Orlando: It's about asking those questions, as you said. They want an expert.

Nelson: They know by the questions I ask them that I am an expert in what I do, so they immediately develop trust.

Orlando: What characteristics make an expert like you in real estate such a success?

Nelson: Developing a rapport. I have the ability to talk to a Fortune 500 CEO, and I have the ability to talk to someone like the lawn guy. I develop rapport with anybody and everybody very quickly. I'm not necessarily there to develop a relationship or friendship with them. I certainly have developed relationships and friendships, but it's not necessary. I'm here to do my job and stick to business as much as possible. Of course, if it turns social, that is great.

Orlando: You've worked with many CEOs and very successful entrepreneurs. Is there anything you've learned from those people in particular that stands out, like the way they handle themselves in terms of business?

Nelson: I certainly try to learn every single day from everybody that I'm around. The biggest room in the world is room for improvement. You can always improve.

Obviously, those CEOs and people at the very top can obviously afford the $20-, $30-, $40-million houses because they are successful. You want to get in front of those people. I ask them questions. These are very sophisticated buyers.

Back at the top of the market in 2005 and 2006, there was only one sale in the city over $20 million, and that was the house I sold at 12 Indian Creek. That was the only house over $20 million! In 2014 we had many houses selling for over $20 million.

Everybody has access to the same information, so you have to be one step ahead of the buyer. You have to know a little bit more than what they know. You must have the knowledge of the market. That's what I sell. By teaching them and educating them on the market, that's how I show them the value of what they're paying for.

Orlando: What's the best advice you have ever received?

Nelson: I was having success in real estate and wanted to possibly branch out into other things, and my father told me one day, "Just stick with what you know. You're very, very good at what you do. You can't be a jack-of-all-trades and master of none, so just stick with what you know, and you'll be successful. If you love what you are doing, why bother going into 10 different other things?"

Orlando: We have saying in coaching that goes like this: "By focusing in one area, you will create many opportunities in other areas."

What piece of advice would you give a real estate agent who is getting started in the business?

Nelson: You have to be very, very knowledgeable of the market and sound very educated. You must know what you're doing when you're in front of the buyer. Again, you usually have very little time in front of the buyer and very little time to impress them.

Orlando: What advice would you give to an experienced real estate agent?

Nelson: I grew up in South Miami, and the only time I used to come to Miami Beach was to go surfing where the Continuum is now. I didn't know Miami Beach, so I literally got in my car with the map and learned the streets. I went to the open houses every single Sunday because when you physically see something, you can describe it much better than you can from photos or virtual tours.

Orlando: Do you still work with buyers only at listing, or do you work only with sellers?

Nelson: No, I work with both, but I try to work with sellers more than buyers because if you have all the listings, you control the market.

Interview #11: Tomas Hoffman

During his 25 years working exclusively with international buyers, Thomas Hoffmann, from Volare Realty, has had years with over $180 million worth of real estate sales. He is one of the most successful and respected international real estate agents in Miami.

Orlando: Tell me about your business life. How long have you been in the business?

Tomas: I have been in real estate for 25 years now.

Orlando: You're very successful in real estate, but you told me your background is in finance. I know you also worked in another industry for many years. Can you share that experience with us?

Tomas: Sure. During the late '80s and '90s, I was involved with what is known as multilevel marketing. This gave me the ability to learn from other people. Although we were not as successful financially as we are in real estate, we developed relationships all over the world, and we developed a level of thinking that we didn't have before. I can tell you that it contributed greatly to our real estate business and was great for improving our real estate results.

Orlando: I know you have mentors. You were speaking to me about one specific mentor. Who was that person?

Tomas: During my lifetime, I have had many people from whom I've learned because very early on in life, I had an attitude of learning, growing, and changing. If you want to have more, you need to evolve and learn. You have to have some role models. You have to find other people who have more knowledge than you do, and you have to be humble enough to be able to learn from them.

I have had several mentors throughout my life, but I remember one specifically. He was the guy who guided most of us during the multilevel marketing processes. His name is Carlos Marin.

Orlando: What did you learn from Carlos?

Tomas: Write this down: In life, you don't get what you want, you only get in life what you focus on. If you want to gain something in life, you've got to focus on that particular result, goal, target, call it whatever you want to call it. Some people call it a dream. You stay focused, you develop a plan, and you stick with the plan.

You don't change the goal, but maybe you have to change the plan. A lot of people put their plan in stone. You want to put your goal in stone and your plan in sand. Technology evolves, people change, circumstances change, politics change, but your goal should never change. You should have developed some dreams and goals that you want to attain. You have to follow those every day.

Orlando: Like any other successful agent, you've learned very important lessons through the years. What is one that you remember, and what did you learn from it?

Tomas: Years ago our market was in a recession period, and you couldn't sell anything. The worst thing that happened was that I had two very good clients—both developers buying land from us—who went under in the same month. That taught me not to have a large part of your business dependent upon a single individual or two individuals or companies.

We really had a hard time because these people were doing millions of dollars of business, and both disappeared over night. All of a sudden, we had no clients. That taught me about diversification.

In our current structure, we deal with different countries. At any given moment, if one country becomes more than 20% of our sales, we start marketing efforts in the other countries. We try to balance our client base as much possible because we don't want to be dependent upon one country or one client, or, like you said, somebody who becomes your employer.

Orlando: What is the number-one piece of advice you would give to an agent, whether they are new or experienced?

Tomas: I would say three things:

1. Follow up. You should do never-ending follow-up.

2. Learn from adversity. You have to learn from adversity in a good way even if you don't like what is happening. At the end of it, you sit down and say, "What did I learn from this experience?"

Usually, I would say that I welcome those challenges these days. I find them interesting. Most people don't.

3. Attitude will determine your altitude. Be ready at all times, dress appropriately, shave, make sure your phone is charged, have a working pen, be ready to pay for parking.

Orlando: Do you have a particular sales technique?

Tomas: Very early in my career I decided to become the expert at what I do. I spend a lot of time doing research. I meet with people from different projects almost on a daily basis. I'm always sharpening my axe, if you will.

I go out and see projects, and I like to know everything about the projects I see. I want to make sure that I know more than everyone about the projects. I know the price points, I know who sells he projects, and I know the terms. This translates to credibility with clients because when you start talking to somebody, they know that you know. You don't have to paint the picture of somebody you're not. You know because you studied and invested the time.

I invest about an hour or two per day just investigating and studying a particular project. I breathe real estate.

Orlando: That's a common trait for most top producers. Most struggling agents say that they don't have time to do that. In coaching, we are very adamant about it. Every single day you have to invest time and money.

Tomas: We invest time, resources, and money.

Orlando: I know you are interested in reading, like myself. Is there any book that you would recommend?

Tomas: We are in the people business, and I think that one of the things that will help you succeed greatly is people skills. Not everybody has people skills. Some people come from different areas of life and have different levels of people skills, but in real estate, you deal with people more than with properties.

The one book that comes to mind that everybody should read is *How to Win Friends and Influence People*. It's an oldie from Dale Carnegie, but it's the one book that can teach you about human interaction. If you want to grow your financial mind, read Robert Kiyosaki's *Rich Dad, Poor Dad*. I was shocked when I read that book. I realized what was going on.

Orlando: His second book was even better: *The Cashflow Quadrant*.

I'm an avid reader. I make it a point to read at least 15 minutes a day. When you read for 15 minutes, you usually keep going. Sometimes you end up reading for 30 or 40 minutes, but at least you do 15 minutes a day. There's a saying that says, "Five years from now, you will be the same person as you are today, with the exception of the people you meet and the books you read."

You said something before the interview that I had never heard before: Books will tell you things that other people won't tell you or that you won't accept. Explain that.

Tomas: Books have the capacity to open up your mind. When you're reading, you allow information to come into your mind that you would not accept from another human being. It's very interesting because you allow the book to come in and make you grow.

Sometimes in our business, we can influence people in a good way by giving them a book. If I told somebody, "You have to change this or that about yourself," most people would shoot me down or not accept the information. However, if I gave them a book, and the book told them the same thing, they would accept it in a different way. It's an interesting concept.

Orlando: Imagine what kind of person you could become if you read a book a month or a book a week?

Tomas: Most people think that success means acquiring something or getting somewhere. The reality is, you learn with time and experience. Real success, to me, is the pursuit of success. It's waking up every day and feeling good about what you do, learning and being in the pursuit of success.

Orlando: Can you give a final piece of advice to a new agent?

Tomas: If you are a new agent, what you need to do first is acquire all the knowledge and training. You must be willing to invest in your education.

Second, you need to make a list of at least 100 names, and then pick up the phone and say to them, "If I can be of any help to you or to anybody you know, I am here to serve you and to help you buy or sell real estate."

If you say that to100 people, trust me, you are going to run into somebody who will know somebody or who is currently interested in buying or selling.

Orlando: In coaching we say that the most important part of your business is your database and learning how to nurture and grow your list. A significant aspect of your business is building that database, but, more importantly, it's strengthening the relationship with that database. You need a system for that.

Tomas: If you, as an agent, have been in the business for 10 years or more, you need to stay in touch with technology. Don't fall behind. When many agents become experienced, they fall behind the technology. You may think it's not important, but it's very important because the mainstream is going that way.

Finally, if you want to attain a high level of sales, you must learn how to build a team. You only have 24 hours a day, and you can only do so much, but once you learn to build a team and to leverage yourself, that may be the pivotal point in your business. Initially, just start with an assistant or maybe some junior agents who work with you, but in some shape or form, you have to develop a team. You can't be successful without a team.

Orlando: When we work with top producers in coaching, that is the first thing we address. It is a three-step process. First is profitability; once you are profitable, you need to go to step two, which is systems. For that you need a team. Step three is scaling your business, and there is no way you can do that without a team.

Tomas: I work fewer hours today than I ever have and produce more money than I ever have, not because I am smarter but because I have a team.

Paul Gary, the richest man in the world in the 1940s, said, "I prefer 1% of the efforts of 100 people than 100% of my own." That quote stuck with me because that's leveraging yourself and your knowledge.

Interview #12: Riley Smith

Riley Smith is a top producer for EWM. He sold 121 properties in 2014 and did over $70 million in sales.

Riley Smith is in the top 1/2 of 1% of Realtors in the country. He has also earned the distinction of selling the highest number of homes in Coconut Grove for over 6 years.

Riley and his team sold almost 3 times as many homes as the second most productive agent in Coconut Grove in 2015.

Orlando: What's your background, Riley?

Riley: I was a floundering sales person. I tried many things, including selling washers and dryers and helping charities raise money. I didn't find my own way for a long time. I didn't have a career path right after college. I think that's probably a common thread with REALTORS®. We tend to come to this business after we've tried a bunch of others.

Orlando: Why real estate? How did you get involved in the business?

Riley: I got involved with real estate because of my best friend. He was a REALTOR®, and I wanted to buy a house. I said to him, "I have this much money."

He laughed at me and said, "You want to buy in Coconut Grove with that?"

I said, "Well, there are two houses." He didn't even leave his office because he thought I was joking.

I got in my car and drove to the first one. The owner was standing outside. I asked to see his house and went in. I liked it.

I went back to my friend's office and said, "I would like to buy this house." Thirty days later, we were closed. I looked at the closing statement and saw that my friend had made $20,000 dollars.

I said "Oh my god, this is the easiest business in the world. Let me get my license."

Orlando: That was 14 years ago. Did you have a mentor when you got started in the business?

Riley: Yes, I started with Coldwell Banker 14 years ago and Ivory Cooks, who is a sort of a local real estate legend here in the Grove. After watching me flounder for a while, I went to him and said, "What am I doing wrong?"

He started laughing and wrote a long list. It was overwhelming. He started with, "Maybe you should not go to the beach every day; instead, come in to the office."

He really took the time to teach me how to be a professional and that this is a business. You need to have a plan, be organized, and work hard. I didn't want to hear that, but once I started learning, watching him, and following him around, it started resonating that maybe if I did something a little differently, my business would go in a better direction.

Orlando: You said something extremely important: Real estate is not a job. What we teach in coaching is that this is not a job or a career; this is a business, and in order to make money, you have to think like a business person.

Riley: Most people think real estate is a career and that they can get into it and not spend any money. Tell me what successful business allows you to do that. Once you realize that you have to spend in this business, you start figuring out the right way to do it.

Orlando: You invested time, money, and effort into building a community by educating clients in the area with a blog. When I first talked to you on the phone, I told you that I thought your story was so interesting because you jumpstarted your business with a blog when most people didn't believe in blogs.

Riley: At that time, I didn't believe in blogs either. Luckily, I was in the right place at the right time. Beth Butler was our vice president, and she was a very forward-thinking person. She had brought to EWM a representative from a company in California called Jim Cory. She said, "This is going to be the foremost company in real estate blogging."

The name of that company was Real Estate Tomato. I thought that was the dumbest thing I had ever heard in my life. First of all, I'm a better talker than I am a writer, so the idea of writing a blog was overwhelming. I closed my eyes and couldn't wait for him to leave.

Then things started happening. The market changed and got a little tougher. I was just starting my career. I knew I wanted to grow, but I couldn't compete financially with the big agents, so I had to figure out a way to get my message out there, build my brand, and reach clients without spending a lot of money.

The beauty of blogging was that the capital cost was a couple thousand dollars, and the rest was your return, forever. That couple thousand has now turned into millions of dollars in business, but it took a while to take off; it wasn't overnight.

Finally, after about a year, 200 people were reading my blog daily. It started to become a really good marketing tool for us. If you are someone who is disseminating information, people read it and believe you to be the expert. Only an expert would do that, so we started learning how to monopolize on it.

If you Google Coconut Grove, we are all over the place. We never paid to be there; it's all organic.

We've learned that Google has looked to us as a news source. Therefore, they put us higher in the search results. That really jumpstarted our business and was the catalyst that allowed us to then spend money in other areas as we started to grow.

Orlando: When we are coaching agents, we say, "Content is king." It's education-based marketing, and that's exactly what you are doing. You are not telling people that you are a top producer or the most experienced. Instead, you're giving them information. A well-educated client is an easier, faster, cheaper, and better client to work with. By providing that information, you're not only becoming an expert, you're positioning yourself as an expert, as you said, in "a less expensive way."

Riley: We have written over 1,200 blog posts. We post about every other day on a particular site, and now we have five sites.

Orlando: It's impossible not to become an expert, and it's impossible for people to not perceive you as an expert when you are creating so much content.

Riley: We do the research, and then we put it out there. Many of our clients—I work mostly with sellers—call us after reading our website for a long time, and they don't call anybody else.

I don't compete on nearly as many listings because the client has already done their homework on me. When they call me, I know I'll get the listing because I know they've been reading the site. There are a lot of people who call in and say, "I have been reading your site for two or three years. It has been so informative, and now we're ready. Thank you!"

Orlando: The way we say it in our coaching program is that there's one primary reason why people do business with you: trust. If we know that trust is what's going to build our businesses and bring clients, what's the best way to do it?

There are two ways. Number one is to communicate with your client constantly, which is what you're doing. Number two is to send relevant information, which is exactly what you're doing.

You told me before that your business increased by more than 50% every single year for five years. That's tremendous growth.

The second thing we talked about off-camera was not only content but what type of content. You're hyper specialized.

Riley: We like to use the term "hyper-organic local information." You can't be all things to everybody in real estate. Miami is a gigantic city. Our business really took off when we shrunk our model down, stopped running all over the place, and just focused on the one community that mad the most sense. I grew up here, and I love it here. People have known me for years here. The more local we become, the better our business gets.

We really grew by subtraction until we had a serious core base. Now, we're growing slowly by expanding and taking our model of the blog here and using it on Brickell, Key Biscayne, and Coral Gables. We're getting other agents to go and teach our methods in those areas.

Orlando: Is there any particular failure that stands out? What did you learn from that experience?

Riley: I feel like you learn faster from failure. We had gigantic failures. We believe in trying everything, so we spent money in every possible way. Sometimes it works, and sometimes it doesn't.

Some of our past failures may have been spending too much energy on buyers. I realized that I can have 25 listings, but I can't have 25 buyers.

The best failure that I learned from was realizing that I was doing so much on my own and couldn't provide the right service.

Orlando: Can you share a success that stands out and what you learned from it?

Riley: My success has come from building a great team. From that, we have been able to leverage a lot. I couldn't do 121 transactions by myself.

Orlando: What do you think is the key to attracting those agents, other than your reputation?

Riley: Generating the leads. I think most of us are very capable of doing the business, of doing the paperwork, of showing the houses, and taking buyers around. That's something that we all can learn pretty easily, but what we talked about earlier is what separates the big boys: It's the ability to gather good quality leads, and then go from there.

We pass those leads out. We can't be in all places at one time. What attracts them to us is that we have enough business to share.

We also offer them experience and camaraderie. A lot of new agents become isolated, which means they miss out and don't learn as fast. As a group, we're almost like a family. We socialize together, and we take the group away on vacation so that we can communicate.

We believe in the importance of education. Education is everything in this business, and most young agents miss that. I like to say that you should work to learn before you work to earn. Know the contract inside and out, the inventory, and the processes of negotiation. Most agents get their first leads and never look back, just following the next lead and never getting the proper foundation.

Orlando: What are some of the challenges new agents face right now?

Riley: They lack the proper training. I like to tell my team that we don't sell houses; we sell confidence. Also, everybody is becoming part of "the team concept," which is really growing. It is leveraging so much time, energy, and money.

Orlando: Is there any particular habit you have to keep yourself up-to-date and sharp in the marketplace?

Riley: My biggest business habit is goal-writing. I'm a huge believer in goals. If you know where you want to go, then you start the roadmap there. I think of myself as having a real estate business, not being a REALTOR®.

Once I made that switch, I started thinking about how to grow this real estate business. I started in 2007 writing down my goals every day. That reminds you daily where you want to be. As you start to write more and more and see the successes that you have had with your goals, your goals get bigger, you start to push yourself, and you gain the confidence that you're going to get there. I think if you don't dream it, believe it, and write it down, it can't happen.

Orlando: There's a magic connection between the hand and the brain.

Riley: We all tend to overestimate how much we can do in a day and underestimate how much we can do in a year. Most of us forget about our goals because we just get on the wheel every day and forget about the big picture.

When I'm writing my goal, I think about what I have to do today to get there. When I'm tracking the goals, I can see if I need to work harder, work smarter, or spend more money. These things come to you while you are writing your goals. It takes only 15 minutes, it's free, and it will change your life. It has absolutely changed my career and my life.

Orlando: During every real estate seminar I do, whether it's for 50 people, at the association of REALTORS®, or on a national stage, I talk about four things we have to do on a daily basis in order to be successful in real estate:

1. Plan your business.

2. Work on developing your business, your content, etc.

3. Practice your presentation and objections.

4. Review what you learned, so you don't forget it.

Success in real estate is not about showing properties or driving buyers around; it's about planning and executing.

Riley: It's about planning and thinking about your business every day.

Orlando: What's the best advice you've received?

Riley: The best advice I received was to start thinking of myself as a business. Don't just think of yourself as an individual because you will get lost in the whole thing. Think of yourself as a business and how you make business decisions every day.

Orlando: What advice would you give to an experienced agent?

Riley: I think most experienced agents need to slow down a little bit. I know many who have been doing this for 20 or 30 years, but they're in the same place for a long time. I think it's because they get caught up in following clients, and they don't slow down and think about the business. Many experienced agents fall into a trap of just going after the next deal. They're not taking the time to think about getting the next 20 deals and getting better-quality leads. It's about slowing down and thinking about what you're doing.

Orlando: No matter where you are now, you run the risk of being in the same place five years from now if you don't take the time to plan.

Riley: Yes, I think that's really the difference between the very good agents and the great agents. I think the ones who I was aspiring to be and the people that I see ahead of me spent a lot of time doing those things versus just doing the business. We all get caught up in the daily grind of this business, but if you could take some time out to forecast the future and try to figure out how to grow and get more leads in the business, I think that would be the biggest change you could make.

Orlando: I know that you're an avid reader like me. What is one book that you could recommend to our audience?

Riley: It's hard to recommend one. I'd like to suggest a couple books. There are a couple that have really changed the way I think about this business.

We talked about *Goals!* by Brian Tracy. That really helped me start writing my goals down. From there, I read *The Success Principles* by Jack Canfield, the author of the *Chicken Soup...* books. That sort of had stories behind the goals, so then I got to see how it worked for other people in real life. Another one I just read is called, *Six Steps to Seven Figures* by Pat Hiban. I think that book is a great book for people who have been in the business awhile. For someone new to the business, just out of school, it would be a little overwhelming, but if you have been in the business for a long time and you are ready to take that next step and you want to make a million dollars in real estate, that book has a perfect step-by-step process for you. Lastly, if you're a new agent, your bible is *The Millionaire Agent* by Gary Keller of Keller-Williams. It teaches you a little bit of everything.

Orlando: Riley, it's been a true pleasure.

Riley: I really appreciate you coming and thank you very much for the opportunity. I love talking real estate; I'm a real estate junky. I'm going on a vacation next week, and I already have my real estate book to read. Everybody thinks I'm crazy, but it's what I am!

Afterword

I live a lucky life because of the many successful entrepreneurs I know and get to spend time with. Every day, I am in the presence of individuals whose lives and work combine extraordinary optimism, commitment, and value creation to the real estate industry. Their presence energizes me and makes me happy to be alive. As successful and useful as they already are, the best part of their lives lies ahead. Each of them thrives on change, challenge, possibility, and opportunity. Each of them is passionate about making their practice and the real estate industry better. Being surrounded by these outstanding individuals makes it much easier for me to aspire to the same qualities and results in my own life. I love the way they take risk, both financially and professionally, and how they continue to improve on a daily basis.

Over the past 15 years, I've personally coached and interviewed thousands of agents, and 30 of the top agents in the country including #4 and #7 according to Forbes and the Wall Street Journal and I discovered that they all do different things in different ways, but they all do the major things the same way.

- What they don't do?
- They don't do Cold Calls
- They don't call expired listings
- They don't work with For Sale By Owners
- They don't just send postcards

What they do is 100X more powerful than ANY of those things. And even now, hardly anybody understands the strategy.

Successful real estate agents do different things in different ways, but they all do the major things the same way.

We have identified 10 major things they all do the same way:

The 10 things are:

1. Mindset

2. Time management

3. Knowledge

4. Database

5. Presentation and objections

6. Delegation and team work

7. Listings

8. Marketing strategy

9. Systems/planning

10. Financials

That is why we have created the TheRealEstateagentScoreCard find out your score at TheRealEstateAgentScoreCard.com

By using the Real Estate Agent Scorecard, you will be able to grade yourself and identify where you need to improve the most in order to grow your business and make more money.

The Scorecard gives you the 10 ways to measure your business growth.

"That which is measured improves. That which is measured and reported improves exponentially" – Karl Pearson, mathematician and statistician

Professor Pearson, an early 20th-century British mathematician, who is considered the founder of the modern statistical methods that drive current business reporting, is credited with this powerful, simple "law:" "That which is measured improves. That which is measured and reported improves exponentially"

Pearson's Law is now a universal operating principle for continually achieving any kind of progress on the planet for both organizations and individuals.

The Real Estate Scorecard represents an overall set of skills measured by 10 contributing abilities. These abilities measure and report your real estate business progress. When you continually measure yourself against the Scorecard, you improve exponentially.

The Real Estate Agent Scorecard exercise is about choosing and strengthening the abilities that have the biggest possible payoff for you in everything you are doing in your business.

The 10 abilities I've identified, which make up the Scorecard, are the result of sorting through more than 75 different abilities over the past 15 years that I've been coaching, listening to, interviewing, interacting and responding to real estate agents of all backgrounds.

I want to share them with you in this first edition of the book, so you can see that every successful agent we interview has them.

The Real Estate Scorecard

What's your real estate score?

1. MINDSET

Mindset, more than any other factor, will determine the level of success in your real estate business.

Here are a few quotes from these 12 producers about the importance of mindset. Their mental approach to the real estate business has been critical to their success.

"My old manager used to say, 'The only thing that's constant is change, and you better change with it.' We have to change." – John Sandberg

"Don't ever assume that what you're doing now that has created your success is going to create your success in the next season, in the next cycle, or in the next year." – Alicia Cervera

"I learned not to be afraid of that with every challenge comes on opportunity and that they were not opportunities without challenges." – Alicia Cervera

"Getting outside your comfort zone. Whenever you are comfortable doing what you're doing, that's a huge red flag that you need to be doing more. As soon as you get comfortable, figure out how you can make yourself uncomfortable because that's where you grow up." – Alicia Cervera

"...you can't be afraid of trying anything... If it's not illegal or immoral, do it." – Alicia Cervera

"If you can't hear a 'No,' you shouldn't be in this business." – Philip Spiegelman

"I think it's very important to remain calm because when you are calm, you pass that spirit to your buyers." – Alicia Cervera Sr.

"My late father used to say, 'The dark clouds in your life are usually much farther away than they appear.'" – Craig Studnicky

"We put a reservation in 252 units in just two days. Sometimes you just need to think big." – Alicia Cervera

"Nothing is worth wrinkles. If you can't do it with a smile, and if you're going to lose your feminine side and happiness, stop doing it." – Alicia Cervera

"If you think you're going to make more money sitting at home than being in the office, go get another job because that's just not going to happen.' If you're in the office, at least there is the possibility of an opportunity…" – Alicia Cervera

"If you want to be successful, you have to be the first one in and the last one out." – Alicia Cervera

2. TIME MANAGEMENT

After mindset, time management is the most important factor. It doesn't really matter how much you know or what skills you have acquired; if you can't control your time, you can't control your results.

"The key is not to prioritize what is in your schedule, but to schedule your priorities." What you don't do determines what you can do.

"You have to ignore the phone and that day-to-day business in order to sit back and put together a strategic plan that will really help you move forward. I decided that I would take 30 minutes a day to think, and that year I made more money than I ever made in my career up to that point." – Alicia Cervera

3. KNOWLEDGE

"If you think knowledge is expensive, try ignorance for a while." – Derek Bok

"You can get a real estate license without a lot of time or effort, but you can't make money at it without putting in the time, the effort, and the commitment to know your business." – Philip Spiegelman

"I'm a firm believer in coaching. My first coach came in 2002. I had hit a plateau, albeit a pretty good plateau. I couldn't get over selling 100 homes in 1 year.

"Ultimately, I sought out a coach, I engaged with him, and I was able to go from 100 transactions to 170 transactions.

"Even to this day, I have always had a coach, going on 38 years. The bottom line is, with coaching, I get better. There is always something that you can tweak, and it's always made a huge difference in my business and my life.

"That is why I have you, Orlando, as my business and real estate coach." – Anthony Askowitz

"Very early in my career, I decided to become the expert at what I do." – Tomas Hoffmann

"During my lifetime, I have had many people from whom I've learned because very early on in life, I had an attitude of learning, growing, and changing. If you want to have more, you need to evolve and learn. You have to have some role models."
– Tomas Hoffmann

What advice would you give a new agent who is getting started?

"First of all, they should go to as many classes as they can. Second, if they borrow money from their mother or whomever, they should try to get a coach.

"I hired you. I was 15 years in the business, and that's how I met you. This business is so competitive that it is better to have somebody from the outside who is non-emotional and can say, 'This is your strength, and this is what you should do.' It will give you a shortcut because for the cost of coaching or taking classes, it is a great reward."
– Nancy Batchelor

"You must be willing to invest in your education."
– Tomas Hoffman

"If you want to improve you need to go to classes and get a coach." – Nancy Batchelor

"Three things: getting up early, fitness, and product knowledge.

"You have to read a lot. You've got to be a little bit ahead of it, but just reading isn't always going to get you there. You've got to see it. It's hard to sell something you've never seen." – Nancy Batchelor

"For me, it's information. If you're going to compete at a high level, you need to be informed." – Craig Studnicky

"We're selling high-price, luxury real estate to very sophisticated people, who can afford to spend $2 million, $4 million, and $10 million. They aren't coming to the table without some knowledge of what's going on. They know if you are giving them bad information or if you're just not knowledgeable. If you want to compete, and you want to be able deal with people at that level, you have to be prepared." – Philip Spiegelman

"Stay teachable." – John Sandberg

"People often think that time is equal to money, but time is not equal to money. You can't get your time back, and that is so important to recognize. When you go on that listing presentation, you have to hit a home run. Once you get up to bat, you have to be successful, or you lose your time, and you're not making any money." – Anthony Askowitz

"As real estate professionals, it's incumbent upon us to enhance our knowledge all the time through education. Once we have our education, it's through implementation that we achieve success." – Jay Parker

"Don't try to reach for the stars; learn what you have to do, learn about your markets, pick a market that you are familiar with, and study it so you know it like the back of your hand. You cannot be a success in this industry if you don't know what you are talking about. It takes time to learn. You must understand that it takes about 12 months, full-time, to start to get traction in this business. It's the same

with every business that you get into. It takes time to grow." – Jay Parker

"We believe in the importance of education. Education is everything in this business, and most young agents miss that." – Riley Smith

"I like to say that you should work to learn before you work to earn." – Riley Smith

"They lack the proper training. I like to tell my team that we don't sell houses; we sell confidence. But you can't develop the confidence without the proper training." – Riley Smith

What piece of advice would you give to a real estate agent who is getting started in the business?

"You have to be very, very knowledgeable of the market and sound very educated. You must know what you're doing when you're in front of the buyer. Again, you usually have very little time in front of the buyer and very little time to impress them. – Nelson Gonzalez

"The biggest room in the world is room for improvement." – Nelson Gonzalez

"I highly recommend to every new agent to take as many courses as they can and really get themselves to the next level early on; otherwise, they won't be in the business for long." – Jeff Morr

"As an agent, you need to be the industry expert… Don't let your client tell you something about the sale that just happened." – Chris Leavitt

"…find a mentor." – Alicia Cervera

4. DATABASE

"To me, a tenant is a buyer, and a landlord is a seller. If you have the opportunity to build a relationship with them, do it. It will benefit your business in the long run. Contact that tenant after six months, and ask them how they like their property. Contact them at month 10, and ask them if they are going to look for something else or if they want to stay there. First of all, you are preserving your ability to earn a commission again, and second of all, you are building a relationship." – Jay Parker

5. PRESENTATION & OBJECTIONS

"Keep the listing and buying presentation short and simple. No one can remember more than three points." – Philip Crosby.

Make sure you prepare yourself.

"It takes one hour of preparation for each minute of presentation time." – Wayne Burgraff.

"No one ever complains about a speech being too short!" – Ira Hayes

If you want to have highly productive real estate business, you can't spend one hour or two in a listing presentation.

OBJECTIONS

"Regardless of what you do in life both personal and business your long-term ability to achieve will be in direct proportion to your ability to handle,

accept, and overcome the obstacles that most people call objections." – Tom Hopkins

There are only eight objections. You can get a copy of my complete guide to handling objections here: www.MontielOrganization.com/guides.

Objections are the part of the sales process most agents fear for two reasons:

a. Lack of Knowledge

• The agent doesn't know the objections. (Most agents don't even know that there are only eight objections).

• The agent may know what the eight objections are but doesn't know how to answer them.

b. Lack of Practice

The agent may know the answers but does not practice them. Therefore, he is not mentally prepared to answer them automatically.

"The sale is not made in the contact with the client, is won in the preparation." Practice, practice, practice.

6. DELEGATION & TEAMWORK

"In order to grow your business as a real estate owner, broker or agent, you need to understand the importance of having a great team. "One of the key things in life is to go away, to enjoy vacation, but if you don't have a team, you can't go away. Going away is one of the key parts of life and one of my main goals." – Anthony Askowitz

"One of my biggest errors was that I kept team members on the team for way too long because I thought that I could change them. I learned that over time, you hire better. If you get someone for $10 an hour, which is not me, you get a person, but getting a person doesn't mean getting a good person. Sometimes paying a little bit more makes a huge difference… Surround yourself with incredible people. That's what has allowed me to grow to where I am today." – Anthony Askowitz

"My first success goes back to before 2002, when I hired my first assistant. The first thing that elevated my business was hiring someone to organize me. She put things in place for me. I understand that I need A and B to make money.

"It's the same in my house. I don't clean my pool, and I don't cut my grass. I have kids, and I would rather spend time with them doing other things." – Anthony Askowitz

"Finally, if you want to attain a high level of sales, you must learn how to build a teams. You only have 24 hours a day, and you can only do so much, but once you learn to build a team and to leverage yourself, that may be the pivotal point in your business… You can't be successful without a team." – Tomas Hoffman

"I work fewer hours today than I ever have and produce more money than I ever have, not because I am smarter but because I have a team." – Tomas Hoffman

"Paul Gary, the richest man in the world in the 1940s, said, 'I prefer 1% of the efforts of 100 people than 100% of my own.' That quote stuck

with me because that's leveraging yourself and your knowledge." – Tomas Hoffman

"The best failure that I learned from was realizing that I was doing so much on my own and couldn't provide the right service." – Riley Smith

"My success has come from building a great team. From that, we have been able to leverage a lot. I couldn't do 121 transactions by myself." – Riley Smith

What are some of the challenges new agents are facing right now?

"Also, everybody is becoming part of "the team concept," which is really growing. It is leveraging so much time, energy, and money." – Riley Smith

"First of all, to be a successful business owner, you need to know how to delegate. You can't do everything. You need to train people how to do their jobs and then trust them to do their jobs. If they can't do their jobs, you need to replace them with people who can, but you need to be able to share the responsibilities, or you'll explode. That's a very, very big factor in running the business.

"I have somebody who handles the website. I have somebody who handles the website leads, and I have somebody who handles the e-fliers. I have a couple of people who handle the showings. Some people handle the contract work and follow-up. Delegate, and the job gets done. If everybody knows their job, the job gets done…I don't sit at a desk. I'm in restaurants and conference rooms."
– Jeff Morr

"My office is my iPhone. Learn to let go. Trust the people that you work with. If they are not the right people, change them, but don't try to be a control freak and do everything because you'll fail." – Jeff Morr

7. LISTINGS

"My coach showed me that you work with an average buyer for 32 hours and with sellers for about 8. Don't forget about buyers, stick with buyers, work with buyers, but learn how to work with sellers and delegate buyers to some of your team members." – Anthony Askowitz

"I say to my agents, 'Concentrate; focus on your sphere of influence. What is the average time someone sells their house?'

"They say, 'Five, seven years.'

"I say, 'What if it's 10 years? If you know 100 people, that's 10 listings a year, 10 sales.' That is almost one sale per month." – Anthony Askowitz

"The second step is getting listings. Listings are your business. Buyers come and go, and buyers will let you down. Some of my biggest trades have been with buyers, but this is not how you build a business. You build a business with listings— listings you can manage. Listings document that you have weight and that you have a place in the business." – John Sandberg

"Some of our past failures may have been spending too much energy on buyers. I realized that I can have 25 listings, but I can't have 25 buyers." – Riley Smith

"I don't take listings that are overpriced, and I leave about 5% for negotiation. If you price the property right, it's going to sell. If you price it too high to test the market, you are going to fail.

"They say that the third agent is the one that gets lucky. I don't want to be the third agent. I want to be the first agent and make it happen…" – Jeff Morr

8. MARKETING STRATEGY

"Pay attention to the mail that you send…What do I care about the home you just sold last month?"
– Jay Parker

In the down market… *"I doubled my numbers. There was a lot of competition, and keeping that consistency in marketing gave consumers confidence in me. In the last three years, I've almost doubled my numbers every year."* – Nancy Batchelor

"Keeping your consistency in marketing. You can't disappear and then appear again when things are good." – Nancy Batchelor

"In the recession period I increased my marketing and I did better than ever"

"Generating the leads. I think most of us are very capable of doing the business, of doing the paperwork, of showing the houses, and taking buyers around. That's something that we all can learn pretty easily, but what we talked about earlier is what separates the big boys: It's the ability to gather good quality leads, and then go from there."
– Riley Smith

"2005 was not a great year for real estate in South Florida. During that time, I bumped up my marketing and ended up doing better than I have ever done before." – Jeff Morr

"Marketing is the key to longevity in this business." – Jeff Morr

"Top producers are not cheap. Top producers understand the value of spending money to make money. I tell agents, 'Spend $1, and you should get $10 back. You want to make $1 million? Spend $100,000 on marketing. You want to make $5 million? Spend $500,000 in marketing. When you're starting out, spend a $1,000 a month on marketing. That will give you a $120,000 a year.'" – Jeff Morr

"They are just throwing away their money. If you are going to do anything, commit for a year, at least. If it doesn't work after a year, then try something else." – Jeff Morr

"I recommend that 20% of your income go back to your marketing." – Jeff Morr

"My database receives a couple of e-fliers a week from me, including market updates, new projects, new listings, and new sales that we have just made. I don't overdo it, but a couple of times a week is okay.

"I do a lot of direct mail because I believe in it. People need to see you, so staying in touch and cultivating referrals and future business is super important.

"You need to be out there. I am a full-time social media person. I understand that costs money, but it's an investment. I am not telling agents to start out spending $10,000 or $20,000 a month. Spend

something thought, and always invest 20% back into marketing. Build it up. Make sure that your two is better than your one and your three is better than your two, and recessions won't matter because when times are not good, sellers have to entrust their listings to the best REALTORS®. Ten percent of the people make 90% of the money in this business. If you're not going to be in the 10%, don't be in the business." – Jeff Morr

"It takes money to make money. Invest money back into marketing." – Jeff Morr

"As we all know; you can't sell anything that you don't market first. This is a sales and marketing organization." – Alicia Cervera

9. SYSTEMS/PLANNING

If you could give one piece of advice to a new agent, what would it be?

"Set up systems in your business. Put everything in place, and get it done now. You will reap the benefits tomorrow. If you plant the seeds today, in six months to one year, you will see the benefits of what you did today. Don't take shortcuts. Do it, and you will be much more successful down the road." – Anthony Askowitz

"I also learned from my Chairman, Howard Lorber, about the importance of planning and how to manage expectations." – Jay Parker

"In life you don't get what you want, you only get in life what you focus on. If you want to gain something in life, you've got to focus on that particular result, goal, target, call it whatever you

want to call it. Some people call it a dream. You stay focused, you develop a plan, and you stick with the plan.

"You don't change the goal, but maybe you have to change the plan. A lot of people put their plan in stone. You want to put your goal in stone and your plan in sand. Technology evolves, people change, circumstances change, politics change, but your goal should never change. You should have developed some dreams and goals that you want to attain. You have to follow those every day."
– Tomas Hoffman

I loved when John Sandberg said, "Success leaves clues. I see a lot of new agents who have all these ideas, like they're going to deal only with royal families or $10 million properties. That's fantastic, but they fail.

"Successful people in our business do the major things all the same way. When we are new, we want to come up with all of these creative ideas when we don't know what we are doing. It's a recipe for disaster."

Make sure you first implement a proven system. Then, with the money you make by working with a proven system and executing on a proven, solid plan, you can start innovating about new ways to get more deals.

"My biggest business habit is goal-writing. I'm a huge believer in goals. If you know where you want to go, then you start the roadmap there. I think of myself as having a real estate business, not being a REALTOR®." – Riley Smith

"Once I made that switch, I started thinking about how to grow this real estate business. I started in 2007 writing down my goals every day. That reminds you daily where you want to be. As you start to write more and more and see the successes that you have had with your goals, your goals get bigger, you start to push yourself, and you gain the confidence that you're going to get there. I think if you don't dream it, believe it, and write it down, it can't happen." – Riley Smith

Orlando Montiel: There's a magic connection between the hand and the brain.

"We all tend to overestimate how much we can do in a day and underestimate how much we can do in a year." – Riley Smith

What's the best advice you've received?

"The best advice I received was to start thinking of myself as a business. Don't just think of yourself as an individual because you will get lost in the whole thing. Think of yourself as a business and how you make business decisions every day." – Riley Smith

"You can't just think about what you are going to do tomorrow. You need to have a plan." – Darin Tansey

"I remember a story about Bill Gates as a child. He would sit in his attic for hours. His mother said that she would go nuts because he was sitting in the attic with the lights off. One day she finally couldn't take it anymore, so she went up there and said, 'What are you doing?'

"He said, 'I am thinking, Mom. Don't you ever think?'" – Alicia Cervera

10. FINANCIALS

"The sophisticated agent asks himself after getting a big commission, 'How much of it am I going to allocate to marketing and branding?'" – Jay Parker

"I tell people that you shouldn't be going into this business if you can't afford to be in it. It's a commission-based business... We try to help people execute when they follow a plan, but they have to be prepared to take that risk and invest in themselves." – Jay Parker

"You must be willing to invest in your education." – Tomas Hoffman

"Most people think real estate is a career and that they can get into it and not spend any money. Tell me what successful business allows you to do that. Once you realize that you have to spend in this business, you start figuring out the right way to do it." – Riley Smith

"...a lot of agents don't know the market or are afraid to spend money on marketing." – Jeff Morr

If you could give one piece of advice to a new agent and to an experienced agent, what would it be?

"Don't be cheap." – Jeff Morr

The Montiel Organization Real Estate Training Program

The Montiel Organization is known as one of leading training organizations for real estate agents and brokers in North America. The organization remains as the most innovative in terms of its ability to help its members exponentially grow their real estate businesses. It was founded in 2008 under the principle and mission of helping real estate agents set their businesses for profit, automation, and growth and reach their lifestyle goals.

Today, The Montiel Organization members not only significantly increase their incomes and free time, they build strong, future-focused teams and practices that outperform their competition. Because of these results, most members continue in the program year after year.

The company continues to grow and enrich its offerings to it members. Headquartered in one of the epicenters of real estate in the U.S., Miami, Florida, The Montiel Organization currently serves over 1,700 successful and highly motivated real estate agents from North, Central, and South America.

"We set out to revolutionize and democratize education for real estate agents by offering unlimited access to hundreds of hours of the highest quality of real estate instruction. We want you to get the world's best real estate education at the world's best price" Orlando Montiel

If you would like more information about The Montiel Organization and its programs for real estate agents at all levels of success, please call 305-305-5965, or visit **www.MontielOrganization.com**.

Here's How to Build a Remarkable Real Estate Business

Over the past 15 years, I've personally coached and interviewed thousands of agents, and 30 of the top agents in the country including #4 and #7 according to *Forbes* and *The Wall Street Journal* and I discovered that they all do different things in different ways, but they all do the major things the same way.

Let's start with what they don't do...

- They don't do Cold Calls

- They don't call expired listings

- They don't work with For Sale By Owners

- They don't just send postcards

What they do is 100X more powerful than ANY of those things. And even now, hardly anybody understands the strategy.

This book is where THE TOP PRODUCERS OF THE REAL ESTATE INDUSTRY share their secrets to achieving massive success. This is the advice you wish you heard years ago.

Be prepared and take notes as we explore the habits and routines of the top producers of the real estate industry.

If you'd like a real breakthrough, build a remarkable real estate business and work like the pros do, we can help you, just visit:
www.RealEstateAgentScorecard.com to get started.